James Francis Hogan

The sister dominions

through Canada to Australia by the new imperial highway

James Francis Hogan

The sister dominions
through Canada to Australia by the new imperial highway

ISBN/EAN: 9783744744669

Printed in Europe, USA, Canada, Australia, Japan

Cover: Foto ©Andreas Hilbeck / pixelio.de

More available books at **www.hansebooks.com**

ADVERTISEMENTS.

The COLONIAL COLLEGE
AND
TRAINING FARMS, Ltd.,
HOLLESLEY BAY, SUFFOLK.

FOUNDED in January 1887, under the auspices of Agents-General for the Colonies, leading Members of the Royal Colonial Institute, the Head Masters of Eton, Westminster, Shrewsbury, Marlborough, Clifton, Haileybury, and other distinguished persons.

The College is situated on its own beautiful estate by the seaside. A most invigorating climate, dry air and soil, and splendid facilities for bathing, boating, &c., tend in the highest degree to promote the physical development of its Students.

Farms of over 1800 acres are carried on by the College for the instruction of its Students, who thus have unrivalled facilities for becoming practically, as well as theoretically, acquainted with all branches of Agriculture, and with Horse, Cattle and Sheep Breeding, &c., on a large scale.

Instruction is also regularly given in Dairying, Veterinary Science and Practice, Chemistry, Geology and Mineralogy, Forestry, Horticulture, Land Surveying and Building Construction, Book-keeping, Engineer's, Smith's, Carpenter's, Wheelwright's, and Harnessmaker's Work, Riding, Ambulance, and various other subjects necessary to the young Colonist.

Many Students from the Colonies and from foreign countries, as well as English Public School and University men, have passed through the College, and are now settled in all parts of the world.

The work of the Institution has been periodically recognised as of great value by Statesmen of the highest rank at home and in the Colonies.

Prospectus may be obtained from the Director at above address, or from the London Office, 6, Victoria Street (adjoining Westminster Palace Hotel), S.W.

A 2

THE AUSTRALIAN IRRIGATION COLONIES

(MILDURA, VICTORIA; and RENMARK, SOUTH AUSTRALIA, on the RIVER MURRAY.

CHAFFEY BROS., LIMITED.

Land may be acquired by intending settlers or absentee proprietors at £25 per acre, payable (if desired) by instalments extending over five or ten years.

In the case of an absentee owner the Company undertake the cultivation and development of the land purchased, charging only a small percentage on the actual outlay.

The climate and soil are pre-eminently adapted for intense culture with irrigation. The Orange, Lemon, Grape, Fig, Pear, Peach, Apricot, Plum, Apple, Olive, and other fruits, with every table esculent, may be grown to perfection.

The *MELBOURNE ARGUS* reports:—"Between Chaffeys and the Settlers an enormous work has been accomplished. The original wilderness of five years ago has been transformed into a charming country of well-ordered orchards and vineyards. . . . Altogether it may be reckoned that fully a million of money has been laid out in the Settlement" (of Mildura alone).

The *TIMES* Special Correspondent in Australia, in April and May, 1893, referred to "the great enterprise at Mildura" and the advantages of irrigation generally. The following are extracts from letters:—"What I have had to say has, I hope, made it clear not only that the country districts are perfectly sound, but that they offer an outlet for English as well as Victorian enterprise. . . . Crops grown under irrigation are so heavy as to double and treble the value of the land. . . . The profits of an orchard or vineyard at present prices are very high."

FROM LATEST PROGRESS REPORT:—

At the Mildura Settlement, where upwards of 10,000 acres of land are already under cultivation by irrigation; being thus transformed from an arid country into thriving and beautiful orchards; the first substantial return yet made (the last season's) amounting to £45,000, or about thirty per cent. on the outlay, which is productively remunerative, made by the settlers up to the present time. It is anticipated that the gross value of the products for the ensuing season will be more than double the above amount. At a recent Intercolonial Fruit Growers' Association's Citrus Fair, held at Mildura, there was a magnificent display of fruits and vegetable products in great variety. It was admitted by the judges that the display of oranges and lemons of Mildura growth was the finest that had been made in Australia.

During the past year Mildura has been visited by prominent men from Europe, the United States, and the Australian Colonies, including some of the most distinguished horticulturists, etc., who have freely expressed and published highly favourable opinions of its progress and prospects in the columns of the leading papers.

The Renmark Colony has been developed up to the present time to the extent of about one-fourth that of Mildura, but it is contemplated to devote special efforts to bringing this South Australian irrigation colony up to the same point of progress within a short period.

London Offices:
CORNWALL BUILDINGS, 35, QUEEN VICTORIA ST., LONDON, E.C.
J. E. MATTHEW VINCENT, Chief Commissioner.

THE SISTER DOMINIONS

Through Canada to Australia by the new Imperial Highway

BY

JAMES FRANCIS HOGAN, M.P.

AUTHOR OF "THE IRISH IN AUSTRALIA," "THE LOST EXPLORER,"
"ROBERT LOWE, VISCOUNT SHERBROOKE,"
"THE CONVICT KING," ETC.

LONDON
WARD AND DOWNEY
Limited
12 YORK BUILDINGS, ADELPHI, W.C.
1896

[*All rights reserved*]

CONTENTS.

	PAGE
INTRODUCTION	1
I.—THE OCEAN FERRY	31
II.—IN A CATHOLIC CITY	36
III.—A COLOSSAL CONVENT	47
IV.—IN THE CANADIAN CAPITAL	59
V.—THE QUEEN CITY	71
VI.—THE METROPOLIS OF MANITOBA	77
VII.—THE PRAIRIE PROVINCE	84
VIII.—OVER THE ROCKIES	91
IX.—THE NEWEST REPUBLIC	98
X.—A CROWN COLONY	106
XI.—THE CENTENNIAL CITY	112
XII.—THE AUSTRALIAN G.O.M.	119
XIII.—PREMIERS, PAST AND PRESENT	128
XIV.—RELIGIOUS SYDNEY	135
XV.—THEATRICAL SYDNEY	143
XVI.—A CITY OF FALLEN GREATNESS	150
XVII.—THREE "BOSS BOOMERS"	157
XVIII.—THE PARLIAMENT OF VICTORIA	164
XIX.—LITERARY MELBOURNE	172
XX.—RELIGIOUS MELBOURNE	180
XXI.—THEATRICAL MELBOURNE	187
XXII.—SOME MELBOURNE NOTABILITIES	195
XXIII—SOME MELBOURNE INSTITUTIONS	203
XXIV.—SPORT IN THE SOUTHERN HEMISPHERE	210
XXV.—A COUPLE OF GOLDEN CITIES	217
XXVI.—AUSTRALIAN FACTS AND PROSPECTS	223
INDEX	232

INTRODUCTION.

AFTER a continuous residence of seven years in London, I utilized the last Parliamentary recess to revisit the section of Greater Britain in which nearly the whole of my previous life had been passed. In addition to the personal desire to meet old friends, revive old memories, and bring my colonial knowledge up to date, I was specially anxious to see and investigate for myself the serious and even startling changes that, according to report, had come over the face of the Antipodean colonies since my departure. Australian visitors had brought to London lurid and sensational accounts of the ruin and desolation that had been brought upon Melbourne by the land-boom mania and its after-consequences, while the effects of the financial crisis and banking collapse of 1893 all over Australia were depicted in hardly less vivid and disquieting colours. How far these reports represented the reality of things, and how far they were the outcome of panic-stricken excitement, was what I principally wished to ascertain. I elected to travel by the new Canadian route, along that great

B

Imperial highway which has recently been opened up by the liberality of the Government of the Dominion, in association with the energy and enterprise of one of the leading Australian shipowners, Mr. James Huddart. As a result of this happy and potential combination, it will soon be possible to run a swift mail and passenger service between the Mother Country and her Australasian possessions, without touching an inch of foreign soil, or losing for an instant its distinctively and essentially Imperial stamp or character. Two links of the service are complete, and in full working order—the Canadian Pacific Railway and the line of steamers that Mr. Huddart has established between Vancouver and Sydney—and the remaining third, or Atlantic link, is in rapid process of manufacture. The Government of the Dominion of Canada has guaranteed Mr. Huddart a subsidy of £150,000 per annum for ten years to enable him to establish a fast line of steamers on the Atlantic, as well as the Pacific, and if the Imperial Government can see its way to contribute a subsidy of £75,000, as recommended by Lord Jersey in his report on the proceedings of the Ottawa Conference, the "all-through British service" will be a fully accomplished fact in the early future. On every ground, of principle, patriotism, and policy, the Home Government is called upon to co-operate with the Canadian and Australasian Governments in establishing this invaluable link of inter-Imperial communication on a permanent and mutually satisfactory basis. Apart altogether from sentimental considerations—and it would be a great mistake to underrate the importance of these in a matter vitally affecting the unity and cohesion of the Empire—the obvious value and the peculiar advantages of this route from the standpoint of strategy and Imperial defence, entitle it at the very least to the modest subsidy from the Imperial Exchequer that has been suggested by the Earl of Jersey, after hearing the debate on the subject at the conference of colonial statesmen in the Canadian metropolis.

The Dominion has unquestionably suffered severely in the past from the lack of speedy, direct, and up-to-date steam communication with the Old World. None of the existing lines attempt to compete with the superb "ocean greyhounds" that course across the Atlantic from Liverpool to New York in the space of five or six days. The R.M.S. *Parisian*, on which I was a passenger, is understood to be the fastest and best-equipped steamer in the Canadian service, and yet it took her ten days in fine and favourable weather to cover the distance between the Mersey and Montreal. No doubt it is true, and it was emphasized in a recent correspondence in the *Times*, that steamers must "slow down" in the fog-infested waters around the Straits of Belleisle, and proceed cautiously up the St. Lawrence, but that admission affords no explanation of, or justification for, the grievous loss of time in traversing the open and unimpeded waters of the Atlantic.

From Montreal to Vancouver is a six days' journey by rail from east to west through the vast and impressive expanse of the Canadian Dominion, within almost constant view of all the evidences of progress and advancing settlement, countless farming areas and numerous embryonic cities of the future. Winnipeg, the half-way house in this trans-continental trip, is a large, attractive, and populous city, that was absolutely non-existent when Lord Wolseley camped on the spot, then known as Fort Garry, a far-away outpost of civilization, in 1871, as commander of the force told off for the suppression of the Red River rebel half-breeds. Winnipeg is a characteristic example of the striking progress and prosperity that followed in the wake of the construction of the Canadian Pacific Railway, that beneficent and monumental enterprise which, by bringing the scattered British North American provinces into closer communication and more intimate relationship, pioneered the way for federal union, and contributed more than any other agency to the creation and consolidation of the Canadian Dominion. The final section of the railway is not only a miracle of engineering skill, but also the source of endless delights, for it climbs the Rocky Mountains in the face of seemingly overwhelming obstacles, and in doing so reveals a long and entrancing succession of natural wonders. The sublime and majestic scenery of the Rocky Mountains in Western Canada, embracing all the panoramic succession of sky-piercing peaks, lofty glaciers, foaming torrents, precipitous ravines, and deep-nestling valleys, ought of itself to go a long way towards popularizing the new Imperial highway with tourists *en route* to the Antipodes.

At Vancouver, the western terminus of the Canadian Pacific Railway, and already a city of considerable size and importance, I took passage for Sydney in the R.M.S. *Warrimoo*, one of the comfortable and well-appointed steamships that Mr. Huddart has placed on the Pacific, in fulfilment of his contract with the Canadian and Australasian Governments. The voyage across the Pacific is a pleasing one in every respect, and is agreeably diversified by stoppages at Honolulu, the picturesque metropolis of the Hawaiian group, and Suva, the seat of Government for the Crown colony of Fiji. Amongst my fellow-passengers were several representatives of Canadian firms and manufacturing houses, who had been despatched to Australia to found branches, study the local products and markets, and generally to co-operate in bringing Canada and Australia into closer commercial and fraternal relations. Indeed, in all the principal Canadian centres—Montreal, Ottawa, Toronto, Winnipeg, etc.—I found the prospects of the development of reciprocal trade with Australasia a prominent topic of eager and sympathetic discussion.

Sydney seemed to me but little changed after seven years' absence. There was certainly nothing in the general aspect of the parent city of the Antipodes to corroborate the lugubrious stories of universal colonial collapse that were current in London. The main thoroughfares were as crowded and as busy as ever; the world-famed harbour rejoiced in a forest of shipping; the wharves and wool-stores were roaring hives of industry; extensive building operations were in progress in the very heart of the city; and, in short, there were hardly any superficial indications of exceptional depression, beyond, perhaps, an appreciable increase in the number of idlers and homeless, who, from time immemorial, have been privileged to camp in the Sydney parks and public reserves. Whatever changes were apparent were decidedly changes for the better, notably the wide, well-planned, and well-built thoroughfare that bisects the business quarter of the city, and reveals the architectural beauties of the General Post Office with excellent effect. Previously, this finest of Sydney public buildings—although disfigured to some extent by a series of grotesque attempts at sculpture up to date—was so hemmed in by narrow streets and alleys that it was impossible to see it to advantage from any point of view. This important and eminently desirable civic improvement was effected during the mayoralty of Sir W. P. Manning, and, by the judicious application of the principle of betterment, the new street has been constructed at practically no cost to the city funds. It has been made to pay for itself. Under the energetic *régime* of Sir W. P. Manning (who, by the way, manages the Australian properties of Lord Rosebery, and other titled investors in colonial real estate) a considerable portion of old Sydney has been demolished and rebuilt by municipal decree. Thousands of aged and dilapidated houses have been compulsorily effaced, and new, sanitary, well-built dwellings erected in their stead. The process, though somewhat Czar-like, is delightfully simple and effective. The Mayor and the Corporation officers sally forth from time to time, and wherever they come across houses which they consider to be in hopeless disrepair, or unfit for further human habitation, the order for destruction and re-erection goes forth, and has to be obeyed without a whisper or suggestion of compensation. By this direct and summary course of action, Sir W. P. Manning has largely done for Sydney what Baron Haussmann achieved for the Paris of the Second Empire.

The last general election in New South Wales, of

which Sydney is the metropolis, resulted in the overthrow of Sir George Dibbs and the Protectionists, and the return of the Free Traders to power, under the premiership of the Hon. G. H. Reid, Q.C. Although Mr. Reid had ably led the Free Trade party during the latter portion of the previous Parliament, after the veteran Sir Henry Parkes had retired from the headship of the Opposition, it was generally anticipated that the Hartington-Gladstone precedent would repeat itself, and that the octogenarian statesman would resume office as Premier when his party came into power again. But this prevailing expectation was not realized, and Sir Henry, in consequence, feels not a little chagrined and disappointed. He contributed materially to the Free Trade reaction by his vigorous rallying speeches all over the country during the week preceding the appeal to the constituencies, and it is certainly regrettable that Mr. Reid and himself were unable to agree on a basis of Ministerial co-operation after the victory had been won by their joint efforts. Very early in the course of the interview with which I was favoured by Sir Henry Parkes, I realized that the veteran was distinctly dissatisfied with the unexpected turn that affairs had taken. His severe criticisms upon the Governor (Sir Robert Duff, late member for Banff),* and upon

---

* Since the above was written, the sad news of the sudden death of this amiable gentleman has been received.

the Liberal Government for sending that gentleman to represent Her Majesty in New South Wales, were probably coloured by the incidents attending the formation of Mr. Reid's Ministry. Venerable in mien, keen in glance, with a patriarchal wealth of glossy, white hair, a still massive and unbent frame, and an utterance slow, clear, distinct, and impressive, Sir Henry Parkes, the head of half-a-dozen Ministries and an active participant for more than half a century in the public life of the parent Australian colony, is certainly the most interesting statesman and the most picturesque personality in Greater Britain. Without any of the benefits of a regular education, a Birmingham foundry-hand at eleven, and an ordinary farm labourer after emigrating to Australia in his early manhood, his colonial career is a remarkable example of what can be achieved by constant self-instruction, untiring industry, and unconquerable determination. Fifty years have well nigh passed since he first came prominently before the Sydney public in the capacity of secretary to the election committee that returned Robert Lowe (the late Viscount Sherbrooke) as representative of that city in the local legislature. And when Robert Lowe recrossed the equator to dazzle the House of Commons with glittering paradoxes, to cast eloquent diatribes at the British democracy, to predict all forms of national ruin and disaster if the masses were enfranchised, and to become a very unpleasant thorn in the side of the Liberal party, it was his erstwhile political secretary who soon succeeded him as member for Sydney. Since then Sir Henry Parkes has ever been in the forefront of Australian politics, and has contributed a highly interesting and important chapter to the history of colonial progress. Lowe, who was so abusively anti-democratic in after years in England, was a decided Radical during his Sydney period, and did not disdain to address enthusiastic crowds from the roofs of omnibuses. He was the idol and the exemplar of the Mr. Parkes of half a century ago, but the matured judgment of the Sir Henry of to-day is naturally less reverential and more judicial and discriminating. Lowe, Sir Henry told me, was a man of exceptional oratorical power, immense erudition, and brilliant repartee, but he was deficient in two of the essential elements of greatness. No man could be truly great who was without heart and broad human sympathies. The secret of Mr. Gladstone's wonderful and abiding power and popularity resided in his all-embracing sympathies, his intense humanity, and his eagerly-responsive heart to the cries and claims of the weak, the down-trodden, and the oppressed of every clime. Sir Henry Parkes is a passionate admirer and a devoted disciple of Mr. Gladstone, whom he first met at dinner in the London house of Robert Lowe. There is a book called the "Wit and Wisdom of Lord Beaconsfield," but it is not generally known that Sir Henry Parkes is the author of a similar compilation under the title of "Wise Words of William Ewart Gladstone," in which he manifests a remarkably intimate acquaintance with the voluminous writings and speeches of the retired leader of the Liberal party. He has also found time to produce three volumes of poems, which, although derided by local critics and political opponents, secured him the high honour of Lord Tennyson's friendship and esteem. A series of gracious letters from the late Poet Laureate, and a similar book of correspondence from Carlyle, with whom the foundry lad who grew into a Prime Minister was also a great favourite, constitute two of Sir Henry's most treasured literary possessions. A volume of his impressions of England during a tour in 1862, a bulky collection of speeches, and an autobiographical retrospect of his long and eventful colonial career, are the principal prose works associated with the name of the octogenarian Australian statesman.

Mr. Reid, the new Premier, is an ex-civil servant of the colony whose destinies he has been called upon to guide. He is a man of solid and steady rather than brilliant or striking qualities. He has now his first opportunity of distinction as a constructive statesman, and it remains to be seen how he will turn it to profitable account. Sir G. R. Dibbs, the late Premier, leads a strong Protectionist minority, and a coalition between his forces and the discontented Free Trade following of Sir Henry Parkes was regarded as a not unlikely development when I was in Sydney. Sir George is a colonial giant, brusque in manner, energetic in action, fluent in speech, frank and outspoken on all occasions, and not unduly sensitive to considerations of cast-iron consistency. After figuring for years as the friend and champion of Australian Republicanism, his instantaneous transformation into a full-blown titled Royalist during a recent visit to England filled the ultra-democratic Australian natives with dismay and astonishment. Indeed, but little has been heard of the Australian Republic since he backslided. If Dibbs, they said, cannot be relied upon to resist the blandishments of royalty, who can?

Cardinal Moran has added a new, noteworthy and imposing institution to Sydney in the shape of an immense seminary for the training of Catholic priests for all the Australian colonies. Hitherto the ranks of the colonial Catholic clergy have been almost entirely recruited from the Irish colleges, but in the opinion of the Cardinal Archbishop of Sydney the time has arrived for the colonies to bestir themselves in the direction of developing and educating a local and native priesthood. With that intent his Eminence has erected on a commanding and spacious site near the entrance to Sydney Harbour a large, handsome, and well-equipped college which is a conspicuous landmark for many a mile. At the time of my visit there were fifty-five students in residence, representing all the Antipodean colonies with the sole exception of Western Australia. While resident in the northern hemisphere, Cardinal Moran was an enthusiastic antiquarian, devoting himself in a special manner to the early history of the British and Irish Churches, a subject on which he is recognized as one of the highest of living authorities. During the past few years his Eminence has pursued a similar line of industrious investigation with respect to the early history of the Catholic Church in the colonies, and the results of his researches among the archives of Rome, London, Paris, and Dublin, as well as the various colonial capitals, are about to be given to the world in a couple of illustrated volumes, to be published simultaneously in Sydney, New York, and London.

Up to quite a recent period there was a constant and vigorous rivalry between Sydney and Melbourne, each claiming to be the "queen-city of the southern hemisphere." But, for the present, at least, that contest for supremacy is at an end. The ascendancy of Sydney in respect to population, commercial pre-eminence, and shipping activity, is clear and unmistakable to the most casual eye. Melbourne's retrogression, stagnation, collapse—call it what you will—is no less striking and manifest. As I walked through the streets of the Victorian metropolis, after an absence of seven years, and beheld the startling and dismal change that had come over the scene—the desolate aspect of once prosperous thoroughfares, the host of untenanted offices and shops, the wilderness of derelict houses in the suburbs, the utter absence of all the former abounding life and energy, and the general suggestion of deep depression and departed greatness—I found myself mentally ejaculating, "The London stories were true, after all." But I do not for a moment believe that the progress of Melbourne has been permanently arrested, although the accents of despair are now very frequently, too frequently altogether, on the lips of her citizens. Melbourne has, undoubtedly, received a severe shock, and has been thrown back in the race for several years, but there is no earthly reason why the capital of a colony like Victoria, possessing such a variety of undeveloped mineral and vegetable resources, should not be able to retrieve the errors of the past and recover no small portion of her former prosperity. Melbourne is now paying the penalty for indulging in a season of insane and unbridled dissipation on her own account, in addition to sharing the general load of misfortune that has been brought on the colony at large by years of disastrous legislation and ruinous extravagance on the part of successive Governments. The more immediate and responsible cause of the present afflicted condition of Melbourne is to be traced to the reckless and unprecedented land-boom, which commenced there in 1888, and led to a saturnalia of wild speculation that literally demoralized the whole community, and brought untold evils in its train. Suburban lands were artfully forced up by interested individuals to nominal prices that were a hundred, and even a thousand times in excess of their real value; syndicates were formed in all directions for the acquisition, the sub-division and re-selling, at an enormous profit, of desirable estates; people bought lands and properties in the morning and sold them again early in the afternoon at an advance of thousands of pounds; eligible corner blocks were secured in the business quarter of the city, and on them were rapidly erected huge many-storied edifices, that in their desolate emptiness stand to-day as ghastly monuments of human folly and short-sighted credulity; scores of mushroom banks and financial corporations were swiftly generated in the noisome soil of universal speculation; a number of new, and now mostly unoccupied, suburbs of vast extent sprang into being under the fostering influence and patronage of rashly-adventurous building societies, determined to make hay while the land-boom sun was shining; even the old-established conservative banks, after resisting the temptation for a while, found the intoxicating atmosphere of excitement too much for them, and plunged headlong into the whirlpool; a veritable mania took possession of all grades and classes in the community, and everybody was making a colossal fortune—on paper.

Of course there could be but one inevitable ending to all this senseless, clamorous, and well-nigh universal gambling in fictitious land-values. Such an immense superstructure of reckless speculation, built up from a foundation of fraud, deceit, villainy, sharp practice, and unscrupulous devices of every conceivable description, was bound to topple over sooner or later, and overwhelm all who were not lucky or far-seeing enough to "stand from under" in time. When the gigantic bubble did burst, the consequences that ensued were deplorable in the extreme, involving the degradation and ruin of public men of the highest standing, who were amongst the most active promoters of the boom, the trial and conviction of an array of bogus bankers, the revelation of an appalling crop of embezzlers and criminal speculators with their employers' money, the failure of a number of the leading building societies, in which the accumulated savings of thousands of thrifty workers had been invested, and—most grievous blow of all—the collapse of nearly all the long-established legitimate banks, by which business was practically paralyzed, the cash of the community locked up, every form of laudable enterprise brought to a standstill, and an era of panic-stricken distrust and general loss of confidence inaugurated. Land and real estate that had so recently been run up to fabulous prices now became absolutely unsaleable; an exodus of the working population commenced in consequence of the lack of employment, and steadily drained the suburbs of their vitality; the daily lists of "New Insolvents" assumed proportions far beyond all local precedent; unfortunate shareholders in the collapsed banks and financial corporations were in many instances reduced at one stroke from affluence to penury by the necessity of responding to relentless calls; and, in short, the dark pall of deepest depression settled over the "Marvellous Melbourne" of former days, and has not yet appreciably lifted.

On the top of the local misfortunes that have just been enumerated, and which Melbourne may not uncharitably be said to have largely brought upon her own head, were piled the additional disastrous consequences that resulted from the serious condition into which the general finances of the colony had been allowed to drift. Melbourne, as containing within its limits more than a third of the inhabitants of Victoria, would necessarily suffer most from the mistakes, the deficiencies, and the incompetent management of the central Government. Excessive borrowing, and the reckless dissipation of the capital thus acquired, are responsible to no small extent for the serious financial situation in which Victoria now stands. Million after million has been raised in London, until the public indebtedness of the colony has reached the formidable figure of fifty millions, the periodical nterest on which represents a heavy drain upon the diminishing local revenues. If this immense amount of borrowed money had been carefully and reproductively expended, the colony might have had little or no reason to regret having borrowed to so large and injudicious an extent, but unfortunately it has been too often sunk in the construction of erratic and unremunerative railways undertaken for political and party ends; the erection of numerous ornate and wholly unnecessary public buildings in every city and town, also to oblige and conciliate the local member; the building of elaborate and costly defence works that are ludicrously out of proportion to the people and property they are supposed to protect; and the multiplication of Government schools all over the colony, in pursuance of the idiotic craze for ultra-secular teaching that has so disastrously dominated the State system of primary instruction in Victoria during the past twenty years. Millions would have been saved, and one-half of those expensive schools would never have been required if the State, instead of insisting so arbitrarily upon, and clinging so tenaciously to, the policy of godless education, had accepted the fair, just and reasonable compromise of recognizing the voluntary schools, to the extent of paying a capitation rate for the secular instruction imparted in them. Many of the State schools are now being closed, or amalgamated with others, in obedience to the stern decrees of hard times and enforced economy; but that so much public money should have been literally thrown away on a vain attempt to de-Christianize the rising generation, is perhaps the most discreditable and reprehensible feature of the financial difficulty in which Victoria now finds herself.

The enormous extent to which the public service has been crowded with employées by successive Ministries constitutes another very appreciable and important factor of the situation. A careful calculation shows that, on the average, one person out of every twenty in Victoria is in receipt of Government money, and so thoroughly and systematically organized is the large body of public servants that they are practically the masters of the public while nominally servants, and undisguisedly control the fate of Ministers and Ministries. At the last general election the

Government of Sir James Patterson was defeated and overthrown avowedly by the votes and political influence of the public servants, because Sir James had made stern and rigorous retrenchment in the Civil Service a cardinal feature of his policy.

Mr. Turner, who succeeded Sir James in the premiership, naturally refrained from grasping the nettle of retrenchment as long as he possibly could, but he has been forced by the desperate condition of the finances into taking up the policy of his predecessors in this respect, and striving his utmost to reduce the vast and extravagant army of Victorian civil servants to reasonable and economical proportions. Whether he will thus succeed in lightening the decks of the Victorian ship of State, and navigating her into smooth financial waters, the course of events during the current year will enable us to judge. I had the pleasure of hearing Mr. Turner deliver his first financial statement in the Parliament Houses at Melbourne, an elaborate architectural pile which cost a million of money in construction, and is not the least shocking example of the reckless, unbridled extravagance that has so largely contributed to bringing the colony into its present pecuniary straits and embarrassments. Mr. Turner is an amiable, courteous, fluent, intelligent, and well-meaning member of the lower branch of the legal profession; but he has had no practical experience of financial administration, and, while wishing him every success in the herculean task which he has undertaken, I cannot dispel a doubt that he is hardly strong and commanding enough to cope successfully and satisfactorily with the very difficult and exacting situation that has arisen in Victoria. The plain fact is that the colony was never so deficient in sound, clear-sighted, and well-informed statesmanship as at present. Previous Victorian Parliaments possessed men of the highest capacity and qualifications: Sir William Stawell, Sir John O'Shanassy, Sir Charles Gavan Duffy, Sir George Verdon, Sir James McCulloch, Sir Archibald Michie, Sir Andrew Clarke, the Hon. George Higinbotham, the Hon. Peter Lalor, and their contemporaries; but they are now either dead or retired from public life, and the new generation of Parliamentarians, with one or two exceptions, have so far not evinced the possession of the statesmanlike character, insight, and ability that distinguished their predecessors. A strong, capable, and practical financier is the crying need of the hour in Victoria, and in view of the dangerous delay in developing one on the spot, the colony is to be sincerely congratulated on the appointment of Lord Brassey as its new Governor. True, the Governor of an autonomous colony is debarred from official interference in its party politics or its financial concerns, but under the very exceptional circumstances of the case, the advice and suggestions of such a shrewd, sensible, level-headed, experienced, and successful man of business as Lord

Brassey, will assuredly be of the utmost value and assistance to Ministers in rescuing the colony from a humiliating and perilous position. Once the present unpleasant situation is successfully surmounted, the finances placed on a solid and business-like basis, expenditure brought well within the limits of income, and the bloated civil service compressed to its proper and natural bulk, there is no reason why, under careful guidance and the rigorous avoidance of the errors of the past, Victoria should not enter on a revivified career of steady progress and well-ordered prosperity.

At a time when the rival merits and the respective demerits of Local Option and the Gothenburg system of the municipal management of public-houses are being eagerly and energetically canvassed in England, the experience of the colony of Victoria in the matter of temperance reform is both interesting and instructive. The temperance party in Victoria, numerous, active, and well organized, succeeded in carrying a Local Option law through both Houses of Parliament, but they are now bitterly disappointed with its practical working and the smallness of its results, and the Act to all intents and purposes has become a dead letter. It was put into operation in some half-dozen centres of population; the ratepayers voted for the reduction of the public-houses in their respective districts to a certain figure; effect was given to this popular vote by the police authorities, who selected the houses that, in their opinion, it was most desirable to close; and then a judicial tribunal heard all the parties concerned and determined the amount of compensation to be awarded to the owner and the licensee of each of the abolished hotels. It was on this ugly rock of compensation that the Victorian Local Option law has been wrecked. Even the most flourishing of Treasuries—and needless to add, the Victorian Treasury has been the reverse of flourishing during recent years—could not long stand the strain of a Local Option law *plus* State compensation to expropriated owners and licensees. In Victoria it was not only a case of purchasing temperance reform too dearly, but also of getting little or no return for the money. I particularly studied the operation of the Victorian Local Option law in Geelong, a maritime town about forty miles from Melbourne, which has always been a stronghold of the temperance party, and which returned the leader of the Local Optionists, the Hon. James Munro, to Parliament. In this town, one of the oldest settlements in the colony, a score of hotels were summarily closed by the vote of the ratepayers, compensation being awarded to owners and licensees to the aggregate extent of £20,000, but I was assured by a consensus of authoritative information that there was no appreciable diminution of drinking and drunkenness in consequence. The custom was either transferred to the nearest hotels that continued open, or else the legally-closed houses were smartly and quietly converted into "clubs," under which convenient designation they were strongly suspected of surreptitiously carrying on the old trade with the same old patrons, although it was exceedingly difficult to prove the fact and secure a conviction. I am a total abstainer myself, and a thorough believer in temperance reform, but I am bound to say that my observation of the working of Local Option in the colonies does not inspire me with increased enthusiasm for that mode of treating the greatest, the most lamentable and far-reaching of social ills. Local Option has been tried and found wanting in Greater Britain; why not give the Gothenburg system, of the municipal management of the liquor traffic, a fair trial within a limited area, and thus practically test its adaptability to British tastes, habits, and conditions of life?

I paid two visits to Fiji, now the only Crown colony in the Australasian group, and as is usually the case with young colonies still tied to the apron-strings of Mrs. Downing Street, I found much discontent and dissatisfaction amongst the enterprising white men who had settled in that tropical group. They are not yet sufficiently numerous to be entitled to the full measure of self-government that obtains in the neighbouring colonies, but they are numerous, important, and influential enough to claim some mitigation of the present severe type of autocratic rule, and to demand the introduction of the representative element into the Governor's Council. This body is now composed of five of the chief Government officials, and an equal number of unofficial members nominated by the Governor, who presides over the deliberations. There is no apparent reason why the unofficial members should not be freely chosen by the colonists of the group, who are as honourable, enlightened and intelligent a class of men as their brethren on the contiguous Australian continent, from which, indeed, most of them, in the spirit of adventurous enterprise, have emigrated. Although the natives constitute the great majority of the population, no injustice would be done to them by the granting of this first rudimentary concession in self-government to the white settlers. On the contrary, their rights and interests would then be far better conserved and protected than they are under the present dictatorial *régime*. During my stay in Fiji I made careful inquiries into the working of the system of native taxation invented by the present Governor, Sir John Bates Thurston. This system, under which the natives are prohibited from paying their taxes in money, and are compelled to raise a stipulated quantity of vegetable produce for the Government every year, was the subject of discussion, both in the Imperial Parliament and the London Press last year. I raised the question in the House of

Commons, and from trustworthy information placed at my command, expressed the opinion that this peculiar scheme of taxation was practically slavery under the protection of the British flag. Mr. Sydney Buxton, the Under-Secretary for the Colonies, said in reply that the information in the possession of the Colonial Office did not corroborate such a description, and that the system was understood to be working on the whole fairly well. But not one of the leading unofficial white settlers with whom I conversed had a good word to say for the system; on the contrary, they assured me that the terms in which I had characterized it from my place in the House were in no way exaggerated, that the system in its actual working was productive of a number of evils and abuses, that it not infrequently happened that the produce raised by the natives in compliance with the demands of a despotic Government was not collected in proper time, that in consequence of this culpable delay it became useless and unsaleable, and that the unfortunate natives were thereupon compelled to raise a fresh supply of the like quantity—a flagrant injustice, by which they were kept working for the Government during the greater part of the year, and left little or no time for providing for their own necessities. But the most conclusive and damning evidence in this connection is supplied by the official who, by virtue of his peculiar position and his specialized knowledge, is the best qualified to pronounce an authoritative and a decisive opinion on the point at issue. Recently the Governor addressed a circular letter to the leading officials and the most experienced white settlers of the Fijian group, inviting their opinions as to the reasons why the native population was so seriously diminishing in numbers. Many interesting and informing replies were elicited, and they have been collected into a voluminous but valuable Blue-book, which has been locally printed, but has not yet been formally published, pending the requisite official permission of the Secretary of State for the Colonies. I, however, was privileged to peruse a copy in the possession of a prominent citizen of Suva, the Fijian metropolis. Among the officials who responded to the circular was Mr. G. A. Beauclerc, the clerk of native taxes and native accounts, and that gentleman lends the weight of his position and authority to these very striking, suggestive, and significant observations:

"Owing to the continual exactions of the chiefs for their own personal aggrandizement, *added to the preparation of tax produce*, the men are kept in such *continuous servitude* that they have not time to provide sufficient food supplies for their families, or proper dwellings. The women also have to render service, not only when they are free from other cares, but when they are child-bearing, and afterwards, when the nurture and care of their infants demand, but cannot obtain, their full attention. The result of this is that not only are children born debilitated and eventually die young, but others who are born healthy become, through after-neglect, weak and die off."

At a later stage, Mr. Beauclerc further illuminates this dark and discreditable situation by the noteworthy remark that "the native taxation scheme is used by the chiefs as a lever to help them in other levies."

Thus, on the evidence of the official who is most directly and immediately concerned with the practical working of the system, it is impossible to resist the conclusion that the representative of Her Majesty in Fiji is openly and unblushingly allied with the predominant chiefs in keeping the natives in what is little, if at all, distinguishable from a state of absolute slavery, or "continuous servitude," to borrow the apologetic euphemism of Mr. Beauclerc. It is a curious characteristic of the average Englishman, and one that not unjustly exposes the people of Great Britain at times to the charges of cant and hypocrisy from candid Continental critics, that so long as the name of an ugly and abhorrent thing is not mentioned amongst them, its non-existence is complacently assumed, although the facts to the contrary are crying trumpet-tongued in their ears. Ask the ordinary Briton, Does slavery still exist under the protection of the British flag? and he will indignantly reply in the negative. Nevertheless, slavery of a far worse and more reprehensible type than that which formerly prevailed in the Southern States of America is at this moment in full blast in at least two British colonies. But the national conscience is soothed and lulled by the comfortable reflection that the *word* slavery has dropped out of our colloquial vocabularies in relation to Imperial affairs. But the hateful thing itself is to be found within the limits of the British Empire all the while. It has merely changed its cloak or verbal designation. In Queensland it is easily recognizable under the style and title of "recruiting Kanakas for the sugar plantations"; in Fiji it displays its forbidding and degrading lineaments under the transparent guise of a "native taxation scheme," by which natives are not allowed to pay their taxes in money or coin, but are compelled to raise produce from their lands for an indefinite period, and must fill the capacious maw of a Government Treasury before they are at liberty to provide for the necessities of themselves and their families.

The intelligent white settlers of Fiji are looking forward to the federation of the Australian colonies to free them from the autocratic and objectionable system under which they are at present governed. They have been represented by delegates at the preliminary conferences, and, as they cannot very well be admitted to federal union until their political constitution approximates more closely to that of their self-governing neighbours, they have every reason to hope and expect a change for the better in their condition, with the dawning of the Australian Dominion. I was greatly gratified to observe many signs and indications that federation was rapidly becoming a live question in Australia. Popular apathy, hitherto the most formidable obstacle to the progress of the movement, seemed to me to have been appreciably dispelled. I addressed several large and enthusiastic meetings in Victoria in support of federation, and everywhere I found evidences of a more healthy and robust public opinion on the question. Leaders of the movement have been encouraged to renewed exertions in all the colonies, and there are excellent prospects of practical results in the early future. The intimate and regular commercial relations that the Australians have recently established with their Canadian brethren, and the consequent better opportunities of studying the practical working of federation in British America, have contributed largely to the improved prospects of federal union at the Antipodes. Australians now realize more clearly and more generally that federation means economic and efficient administration, a powerful infusion of mutual strength, a solidifying cohesion and compactness, a more thorough and systematic development, and a vastly increased influence in the estimation of the world. Thus there are happily good and solid grounds for the prediction that the century will not close without seeing two Sister Dominions on opposite shores of the Pacific.

THE SISTER DOMINIONS.

I.

THE OCEAN FERRY.

"I would rather spend six months in a respectable gaol than cross the Atlantic again." This amusing observation was made to me by an Irish-American priest when we arrived off Queenstown in May, 1887, after a breezy voyage from New York. Fr. O'D. was making his first trip on the water, paying his first visit to Ireland, and he was a martyr to sea-sickness for nearly the whole of the voyage from New York to the sighting of the Irish coast. I crossed the Atlantic again from Liverpool to Montreal last August, this time in company with three American priests (not one of whom suffered from sea-sickness) and seven nuns belonging to the Order of the Faithful Companions, who also seemed to be excellent sailors. Indeed, there was no excuse for anybody getting sick, for the Atlantic was almost as smooth as the proverbial mill-pond from the beginning to the end of the voyage. The

R.M.S. *Parisian*, on which I travelled, is the finest vessel of the Allan fleet, but none of the numerous steamers running between Great Britain and Canada are equal in speed and attractiveness to the "greyhounds" that race between Liverpool and New York. An enterprising Melbourne man, Mr. James Huddart, intends to revolutionize the steam communication between Canada and the old land by building a fleet of fast steamers that will be second to none on the New York route. Most of my fellow-passengers on the *Parisian* were Canadian and Yankee holiday-makers returning from England and Europe, with a fair sprinkling of Australians getting back to the southern hemisphere by way of Canada. When I crossed the Atlantic in 1887, I had a number of Mormons as companions. This time I was accompanied by some members of the newest and most eccentric of American religions—the "Holy Rollers." You sometimes get into very queer company when you are travelling. As we approached the coast of Newfoundland we sighted two enormous icebergs —one presenting the appearance of a colossal cathedral, with numerous spires glistening in the sunshine; while the other was a huge, towering, shapeless mass, suggestive of ruin and destruction to the luckless ship or steamer that came in contact with it. Beautiful and interesting as icebergs are by day, they become very ugly and dangerous neighbours by night. They constitute, perhaps, the greatest peril of Atlantic navigation, for at night they cannot be discerned, and the crash of the collision, with tons of ice thundering down upon his decks, is often the first intimation of their presence that a captain receives. In foggy weather the danger is intensified, and the only warning of the proximity of icebergs that a navigator is vouchsafed is the sudden coldness of the atmosphere. Whales, too, although they have become somewhat rare during recent years, have not yet been banished from the North Atlantic. I saw one leviathan come to the surface, quite close to the steamer, energetically "blow" for a moment or two, and then disappear into the depths of the ocean.

Perhaps the greatest of the federalizing forces now in active operation within the British Empire is the cheapness and the ease with which the principal Colonies can visit each other, as well as pay their respects to the parental home from time to time. The facilities for travelling all over the Queen's dominions are now so abundant and so accessible that people who twenty years ago would never have dreamed of personally touring the Empire, now think as little of a visit to Australia or Canada as they formerly did of a trip to Margate or Harwich. Similarly, Australians and Canadians now re-visit the Mother Country every year in numbers that would have been considered fabulous a few decades ago, and thus the enormous development of our great steamship companies during recent years, and the wholesome rivalry that has naturally and necessarily sprung up amongst them, are silently but substantially doing the work of Imperial Federation, and doing it more effectively than any number of political leagues aiming at the realization of more or less shadowy ideals. The opinion on board the *Parisian* was universal that Mr. Huddart's spirited project deserved to succeed, for while it was admitted that the Allans had done good service in the past, it had also to be confessed that they had not kept pace with the times, and that Canada had appreciably suffered from the want of a fast steam service to and from the Mother Country. No small share of the conversation amongst the saloon passengers was devoted to a comparison of notes as to the personages seen and the places visited in Great Britain and Ireland. These home-going Canadians were evidently deeply and sincerely interested in the historic memorials of the Old Land and the leading men in the British public life of to-day. They lingered over the recollections of what they had seen and heard, exchanged ideas and opinions, and made it manifest to all within earshot that their interest in all that pertained to British national life was of a singularly keen, patriotic, and intelligent character. Asked whether there was any strength or significance in the movement for the annexation of Canada to the United States, they replied that this so-called "movement" was of the most contemptible and insignificant character, and was not countenanced by a single Canadian of standing or influence. No one, indeed, can mix with Canadians, either on land or sea, without being struck by their deep-seated attachment to the Old Land and its institutions, and their rooted determination to hold fast to their Imperial inheritance. Prominent amongst the passengers on the *Parisian* was Mr. J. G. Colmer, the Secretary to the Canadian High Commissioner in London. Mr. Colmer was the life and soul of the social gaieties of the saloon, and a concert he organized resulted in a contribution of close on £30 to the funds of the Liverpool Seamen's Orphan Institution.

II.

IN A CATHOLIC CITY.

On Friday, August 24th, we entered the broad expanse of the St. Lawrence, running for the greater part of the day within sight of hilly, beautifully-wooded shores, with clearings at intervals, in which villages of the whitewashed houses that are almost universal amongst the French Canadians were seen snugly nestling. Next day we arrived at the grand old historic city of Quebec, the cradle of colonization in Canada, built around a craggy height, down which rivers of blood have streamed during the long and desperate struggle between France and England for supremacy in Canada. England conquered in the end, but had to pay a terrible price for the victory. The last great battle was fought at Quebec, and there the opposing generals, Wolfe and Montcalm, both bit the dust. A national monument to perpetuate their mutual memory now stands on the field where they perished, equal honour being done to the victor and the vanquished. Quebec, being a strong natural fortress, was quickly occupied by the French pioneer settlers. It enabled them to hold their ground against the hostile Indians; it became their great centre of trade and commerce, and developed into the recognized metropolis of New France, as Canada was originally designated. It held this position of pre-eminence for many years, but latterly it has been appreciably retrograding, in consequence of the great advantage given to Montreal by the dredging and deepening of the St. Lawrence. Formerly it was the principal distributing centre of Canada, but now Montreal enjoys that enviable and lucrative distinction. Formerly most of the ships and steamers loaded and discharged at Quebec; now it pays them better to go up the St. Lawrence to Montreal. Still, in spite of this adverse turn of fortune's wheel, Quebec continues to be a large, populous, and important city, and nothing can rob it of its pre-eminence as the most historic and intrinsically interesting of Canadian centres. Irregular, sinuous streets, bordered by quaint old houses, straggle around the base of the precipitous mount, but on the heights overhead an imposing modern city has sprung up, and from the citadel that crowns the whole a splendid prospect of the valley of the St. Lawrence and the surrounding country is obtained.

Eight hours' delightful steaming up the St.

Lawrence, past a constant succession of smiling, prosperous-looking towns and villages, brought us to Montreal, the most populous and commercial of Canadian cities. It is not only populous and commercial, but pre-eminently Catholic—perhaps the most Catholic city on the face of the earth. It has a remarkable and romantic history. Jacques Cartier, the renowned French navigator and discoverer of Canada, rowed up the St. Lawrence as far as the site of Montreal in 1553. It was then occupied by the Indian village of Hochelaga, whose chief and attendant warriors came forth to meet and to greet the first white men they had ever seen. Cartier conciliated the Indians in every possible way, distributed presents amongst them, and soon gained their confidence and goodwill. At his request they accompanied him to the summit of a peak, about a mile and a half distant, from which such a splendid and variegated prospect of river, valley, forest, hill, and island opened out before him, that he was immediately inspired to name the spot "Mount Royal," and, in the abbreviated French form of Montreal, the name was destined to be perpetuated by the great city that grew and developed beneath the mountain on which Cartier delightedly stood. On returning to France, Cartier published a glowing account of his visit to Hochelaga, and strongly recommended it as a most advantageous site for a settlement. But it was not until May 18th, 1642, that Cartier's recommendation was actually carried into effect. On that day there landed at Hochelaga a pioneer band of forty-five colonists, one of whom, a soldier-statesman, the Sieur de Maisonneuve, had been appointed governor of the little colony. He was the first to spring ashore, and, on bended knee, to raise a hymn of praise and thanksgiving. Soon an altar was erected in the open air, and around it there knelt the forty-five pioneers, while the chaplain of the expedition, Fr. Vipond, offered the first Mass in Montreal. After Mass the new settlement was specially dedicated to the Blessed Virgin, and Fr. Vipond preached a prophetic sermon from the parable of the grain of mustard-seed. "Ye are few," he said, "but your work is the work of God. His smile is upon you, and your children shall fill the land." The Iroquois Indians became furiously hostile when they realized that a permanent white settlement was being established in their midst, and throughout the early years of Montreal's existence the settlers had a hard and perilous time in repelling the constant attacks of Indian war parties. But the white men gradually made their footing firm and secure; the Indians exhausted their strength, and ceased to be a standing menace to the community, and Montreal, growing in size and importance, developed into a great centre of the lucrative fur trade with the vast regions of

Western and North-Western America. That trade was the foundation of the fortunes of Montreal, the primal source of the wealth and prosperity of the handsome modern city that we see to-day at the head of navigation in the St. Lawrence.

Marks of its Catholic origin and the distinctively Catholic character of its development are conspicuous on every side in Montreal. Churches are so numerous that Mark Twain, the American humorist, has perpetrated a pleasantry to the effect that "you cannot throw a half-brick in any direction in Montreal without breaking a church window." Another would-be humorist thought he was saying a smart thing when he maliciously observed that "there are a great many saints' days in Montreal, and very few washing days." Needless to say, the latter portion of this impertinent remark is a gratuitous libel. The streets of Montreal are made picturesque by the number of priests and members of the religious orders in their distinctive dress. Nuns, both walking and driving, are also numerous. The streets themselves are largely religious in their nomenclature. The leading thoroughfare is called Notre Dame, and other important streets are named after St. James, St. Paul, St. Catherine, St. Antoine, St. Denis, St. Lawrence, St. Peter, St. Francis Xavier, St. Hubert, St. Helen, etc. The cathedral is the glory of Montreal, and the largest church in America. It is an exact copy, on a reduced scale, of St. Peter's in Rome. It is not yet quite completed, the total cost of construction exceeding a million dollars. The imitation of—

> "The well-proportioned dome,
> The world's just wonder, and even thine, O Rome"—

is remarkably successful and striking. From every point it is the dominating and the most picturesque architectural feature of the city. Notre Dame, at the other end of the city, is a massive and beautiful church of cathedral proportions, seating ten thousand worshippers, and displaying a most artistically decorated interior. The Jesuits occupy a large and imposing block of ecclesiastical and scholastic buildings on an elevated site at the top of Bleury Street. Their church is also a capacious edifice, and is specially attractive by reason of its beautiful mural paintings. The French Jesuits, by the way, have an exceedingly high and honourable record as the pioneers of civilization in Canada. True to the genius of their order and the spirit of their mighty founder, they were amongst the first to penetrate the trackless forests of the Canadian interior, facing countless perils, and enduring terrible privations, while converting the Indians to Christianity, and leading the van of progress and enlightenment in the great North-West of America. The population of Montreal may be practically divided into two main bodies, French Catholics and

Irish Catholics. The latter are principally established in Central Montreal, where they have a large and beautifully-decorated church dedicated to Ireland's patron saint. One of the most eloquent and distinguished of the men of '48, the Hon. Thomas D'Arcy M'Gee, was their leader and Parliamentary representative for many years. Since 1882 they have been represented in the Dominion House of Commons by the Hon. J. J. Curran, Q.C., LL.D., now Solicitor-General of the Dominion. Mr. Curran has been a valuable bulwark both of Irish nationalism and Catholic progress in Canada during the past two decades, and I am personally indebted to him for many kindnesses and much useful information while I was visiting Montreal and Ottawa. In the course of a very interesting historical survey of the rise and progress of the Church in Montreal, his native city, Mr. Curran says:—" To-day the position of the Irish-Catholic community of Montreal and its vicinity is one of influence, power, and prestige. The assessment rolls are evidence of the interest they command, to the extent of millions of dollars. Their hold on commerce and manufactures, their representation in the judiciary, in the Senate and Commons of the Dominion, in the local legislature, at the aldermanic board, in the various offices of trust and emolument connected with public affairs, and their place in the learned professions, by men of their race and creed, leave no room for cavil. Census returns are scarcely needed to establish numerical strength, when not only the throngs that worship at St. Patrick's from early morn until noon at the successive Masses, but the congregations of St. Anne and St. Anthony, St. Gabriel and St. Mary, may be viewed every Sunday, and are the living evidence of how the Irish Catholic population of this great and growing city have increased and multiplied, and preserved the inestimable boon of the faith of their fathers."

Montreal is the headquarters of that great institution which was so largely instrumental in cementing the scattered provinces of British North America into one strong and compact federated Dominion. Without the Canadian Pacific Railway, which connects Halifax in the farthest east on the Atlantic shore with Vancouver in the farthest west on the Pacific coast, the British North American Confederation would certainly not be the potent and praiseworthy reality that it is to-day. The C.P.R., as it is familiarly designated, is now, has been for years, and will be for a long time to come, the dominating factor in the opening up, development, and permanent settlement of the vast interior and North-West of Canada. It has already achieved much in these respects, but there are still many millions of acres within the sphere of its influence to be turned to profitable account, not to mention the mineral wealth that every day is now disclosing along the route of the western section of the railway. The potentialities of progress and development that lie at the doors of the C.P.R. are so vast and so countless that it bids fair to stand in the not distant future at the head of the great railway corporations of the world, while at the same time the Dominion of Canada will consequentially reap all the advantages of a largely-increased population and a regularly rising revenue. Sir William Van Horne is the guiding brain and the governing chief of this colossal railway enterprise. His Dutch ancestry reveals itself in the square-built solidity of his frame, and the expressive character of his keen blue eyes. But there is also a smartness and vivacity about his movements, a shrewdness of perception and promptness of decision, a fluency of speech and raciness of comment, that seem to point to an early apprenticeship and business training amongst the go-ahead people of the neighbouring Republic; and such, indeed, is really the case, for Sir William was brought from Chicago, where he had a lengthened experience of responsible railway management, by the founders of the C.P.R. to take the control of their new trans-continental line and give them the benefit of his accumulated knowledge and experience of railway matters. The wisdom of his selection has been amply demonstrated by the success and prosperity which the C.P.R. has attained under his able and energetic management. After holding the position of general manager for several years, he was promoted to the vice-presidency of the company, and on the retirement of Lord Mount-Stephen he succeeded to the presidency. He is still in the prime of life, and he will in all probability rule the destinies of the C.P.R. for many a year to come. The knighthood recently conferred upon him by the Queen was a well-deserved recognition, not only of his personal merits and achievements, but also of the valuable pioneering and colonizing work that has been done in Canada by the corporation over which he presides.

Sir William has a remarkably efficient and courteous coadjutor in the direction and management of the immense and far-reaching business of the C.P.R. in the person of the vice-president of the company, Mr. T. G. Shaughnessy, the son of an Irish emigrant, and a striking instance of the height to which industry, integrity, and native ability, unaided by friendship, influence, or patronage, may raise their possessor in the new world, where every man has a fair field and no favour. Montreal has built a large array of stone quays for the accommodation of its extensive shipping; and additional testimony to its trading pre-eminence is borne by the number of enormous warehouses and grain elevators that line the river side. A beautiful blue-grey limestone abounds in the neighbourhood, and has been largely used in the construction of the public buildings and the shops in the principal streets. The only objectionable feature about this romantic and peculiarly Catholic city is the system of street locomotion—electric tramcars running continually at a prodigious and dangerous speed through all the leading thoroughfares. This high pressure style of travelling is now the rule in all the chief cities of Canada and the United States, but it is abominable to people who have no desire to be whirled about in such a helter-skelter fashion. A story is told of a Chinaman, just arrived from the Flowery Land, who stood stock still in amazement when he first beheld one of those electric cars tearing through the streets of an American city. He thus soliloquized to himself—"No pushee, no pullee ; go like hellee. Great man Mellican man."

III.

A COLOSSAL CONVENT.

THE greatest and the most interesting of the sights of Montreal is the " Grey Nunnery," which is probably the largest and most populous conventual institution on the face of the globe. This immense establishment, or cluster of affiliated charities, fills one of the finest blocks of the city, and another block belonging to the convent is covered with shops and houses, whose rents enable the good Grey Nuns to carry on their manifold beneficences and charitable activities with a continuity and completeness that might not be attainable without some such regular source of revenue. A mere list of the charities and educational institutions under the constant management and sympathetic supervision of the Grey Nuns of Montreal is sufficient of itself to indicate the enormous area covered by their energetic and self-sacrificing labours. Here are some of the principal charities and educational agencies in this great conventual colony :—St. Joseph's Asylum, for orphan girls ; St. Joseph's

Infant School; St. Patrick's Asylum, for Irish orphan boys and girls; St. Bridget's Asylum, for homeless girls and servants out of situations; the Nazareth Institution, for the blind; the Nazareth Infant School; the Bethlehem Asylum, for orphans of both sexes; the Bethlehem Infant School; the Hospice of St. Charles, for aged and infirm men and women; the Hospital Notre Dame; and the Ophthalmic Hospital. There are 524 professed sisters, and the novices and postulants bring the number up to the grand total of 763.

This colossal convent has a very interesting history of close on two hundred years. Like other phenomenally successful institutions, it was tried in the fire of adversity and calumny during its early struggles for existence. Its foundress was Marie Marguerite Lajemmarais, the daughter of a distinguished Frenchman, who settled in Canada. Educated at the Ursuline Convent in Quebec, and possessing the three attractive accomplishments of beauty, wit, and amiability, she soon commenced to shine in Canadian society, and in her twenty-first year she became the wife of M. François d'Youville, a good-looking young gentleman of high family, who proved a frightful failure as a husband. He went irretrievably to the bad, shamefully neglected his wife, spent his nights habitually with drunken and dissolute companions, and finally killed himself by unbridled dissipation.

A COLOSSAL CONVENT.

Thus after eight years of marital misery, Madame d'Youville was left a widow with two sons. The years of sorrow, suffering, and humiliation that she endured as a patient, sorely-tried and uncomplaining wife, were a probation that admirably fitted her for the great work that she was destined to establish and build up in Montreal. When her two sons went to college to study for the priesthood, she commenced her career of benevolence and good works by clothing herself in a coarse, black garb and systematically visiting the sick and the poor. After a time Father Normant, the then parish priest, and Vicar-General of Montreal, induced three other ladies to join her in the performance of these works of Christian charity. The little community secured a small house, and took possession of it on October 30th, 1738. That was the germ and beginning of the gigantic "Grey Nunnery" that now covers a big block in the city of Montreal.

At all times, and in every quarter of the world, anything in the nature of a new Order of nuns seems to have had a curiously inflammable effect on the popular mind, and to have set many mischievous tongues a-wagging. Even Australia has not been free from manifestations of this painful and peculiar phenomenon. The now well-known and highly-respected Sisters of St. Joseph had to pass through a cruel and slanderous time in South

Australia, the colony of their original foundation. Madame d'Youville and her three companions were no exceptions to the rule. When they first appeared in the streets of Montreal, clad in their distinctive costume of grey—a dress now held in the highest honour and esteem in the self-same city—they were actually hooted and pelted with stones by excited crowds, acting under the influence of some demoniac impulse. It would really seem as if Satan, at times, can persuade Catholics to join him in a determined effort to destroy new agencies for good that are specially obnoxious to him, for Montreal was as Catholic a city then as it is to-day. Amongst the absurd and calumnious charges that were concocted and circulated about the Grey Nuns, and which served as fuel to the popular fury, were accusations of supplying the Indians with strong drink, and indulging in it pretty freely themselves. Considering how much Madame d'Youville had suffered from being tied for eight years to a drunken and dissipated husband, the levelling of such a charge against her simply shows to what lengths of improbability unthinking prejudice and sudden malevolence may go. But even at the height of the persecutions she was not without consolation and encouragement, for three young ladies were inspired to reinforce the oppressed little community at the moment when popular hostility was most bitter and active. Things were beginning to improve, and the Grey Nuns were just emerging from the storm of calumny and insult that their first appearance had excited, when a great misfortune befell them, their humble convent being burnt to the ground on a cold winter's night. Madame d'Youville, the sisters, and the inmates barely escaped with their lives, everything they had in the world having been destroyed by the flames. In this deplorable crisis of their fortunes a Montreal merchant proved a friend in need by placing one of his houses at their disposal, and after a time of great anxiety and uncertainty as to the future, the Grey Nuns found a home again in an old and dilapidated building given to them by the Governor, on condition that they would put it in thorough repair. This was their headquarters for many years to come, and in it they established wards for the reception of aged men and women, invalided soldiers, the victims of incurable diseases, and orphans of both sexes. During the long and sanguinary war between England and France on Canadian soil, the Grey Nuns actively ministered to the wounded on both sides. Indeed, one wing of their convent came to be known as the "Englishman's Ward," from the fact that it was nearly always occupied by wounded English soldiers. In September, 1760, Montreal was invested by an English army of 32,000 men, and the general in command, fancying the convent of the Grey Nuns to be a fortification of some sort, gave the word to open fire upon it. The cannon were being placed in position when a soldier stepped from the ranks, saluted the general, and respectfully informed him that the building in question was not a fort, but a convent, adding that the nuns in residence there had once saved the lives of himself and several of his comrades. The general immediately countermanded the order, and the convent was saved. From the first the Grey Nuns established friendly relations with the Indians, who would never harm them, even when out on the war-path or on a scalp-hunting expedition. A Miss O'Flaherty, who became a Grey Nun herself, was actually rescued from the Indians at the very moment when she was bound to the stake and doomed to a horrible death. When Madame d'Youville passed to her reward on December 23rd, 1771, in the seventieth year of her age, she had the consolation of knowing that her institute had triumphed over all its early difficulties, had lived down popular hostility and slanderous tongues, had been firmly established on a permanent foundation, and would perpetuate the good work which she had commenced for centuries to come.

In 1847, the terrible year of the great Irish famine, the Grey Nuns of Montreal rendered noble and memorable service. Flying from their famine-stricken native land across the Atlantic in thousands, an appalling number of the unfortunate people fell victims to the ship fever, and either found graves in the caverns of the deep, or were cast, more dead than alive, on the shores of the United States and Canada, where, huddled together in extemporized sheds or makeshift hospitals, they presented a picture of afflicted humanity almost without parallel in the history of the world. At this horrible period the Superioress of the Grey Nuns was Sister M'Mullen, an accomplished and wonderfully energetic woman. She soon woke up the Canadian authorities to a sense of their duty, obtained official permission for her nuns to take charge of the sheds, and threw the whole resources of the convent—sisters, novices, and outside helpers —into the work of relieving and saving as many as possible of the fever-stricken immigrants. " Sisters, the plague is contagious. In sending you there I am signing your death-warrant, but you are free to accept or to refuse." In these words Sister M'Mullen addressed the assembled Grey Nuns after returning from her visit to the sheds. Needless to say, they one and all accepted what proved to be the sentence of death for many of them. A considerable proportion of them caught the fever at the sheds, and nobly perished at their posts of duty. Four of the Grey Nuns who went through this terrible ordeal, who caught the fever, but were providentially preserved, still survive, one being the present Superioress-General.

Immense as is the institution, or, rather, the long series of institutions, governed and directed by the Grey Sisters in the chief Canadian city, Montreal by no means monopolizes their Christian and charitable activities. Madame d'Youville's original foundation is now the mother-house of more than a score of similar convents. There are ten in other Canadian centres and nine in the United States. The Grey Sisters, too, were the pioneer nuns of the great North-Western Territories of the Canadian Dominion, where they first established themselves fifty years ago, when there were very few white settlers in these parts, and very many wild Indians. There is preserved at the mother-house in Montreal a very interesting letter from one of the pioneer nuns of the North-West, in which she thus describes her journey over the prairies:— "Our mode of conveyance is an antique cart, with high, wooden wheels, and drawn by an ox. For days we travel through the midst of vast prairies, the bright sky overhead, seas of waving grass as far as the eye can reach, one of nature's primeval forests in the distance, a few streamlets, and finally a river to interrupt our progress. Neither bridge nor boat existing, we must devise means to reach the opposite shore. When the current is strong and the river wide, the men construct a small raft made of the branches of trees. On this raft we and all the baggage are carried across. The frail construction is guided and sent onwards by men swimming on each side. If no wood be found in the vicinity of the river, a cart wheel is taken off a vehicle, a buffalo robe thrown over it, and on this Thetis car we brave Neptune's wrath. A halfbreed or Indian has to draw or push our frail boat forward. If the men of the caravan be not numerous enough, a cord is fastened to the wheel and then to the horns of an ox, the other end is given us to hold and guide our bark to the best of our ability. So long as the weather continues favourable our caravan proceeds onward in this manner, halting each day about sunset. The oxen are then let loose to graze, search is made for fuel, the fire is lighted, the kettle put on, and the evening meal prepared. After the repast, prayers are said, our tent put up, and our beds—a buffalo robe—spread on mother earth. On this *soft* couch we repose as best we may, to rise again at three next morning. The tent is lowered, morning prayers offered up, the men go in search of the oxen, the fire is renewed, the morning meal prepared and eaten. Breakfast over, dishes washed, the fire is carefully extinguished, the order to mount and proceed issued, and our caravan begins another day's journey. On through the boundless solitudes, whose silence is relieved only by the song of the birds, the chirping of the locusts, the murmur of the breeze, the rustling of the leaves, the creaking of the cart-wheels, the call or shout of the drivers, the cracking of their whips as they urge on some weary or stubborn beast. Such is life on the prairies when the sun shines; but when the tempest rages, with the wind blowing, the lightning flashing, the thunder pealing, and the rain pouring in torrents, a halt in the prairie or in the wild woods, under a simple tent that every gust threatens to carry off, and no other bed than a buffalo robe on the wet ground, pleasure is no longer a reality. Even when the weather is fine we are followed, surrounded, swarmed, and literally devoured by the most gluttonous creatures in creation. They stalk about in daylight, they revel during twilight, respect not even the shades of night, yet have the effrontery to sound their own trumpet. I allude to the mosquito, that venomous mite whose sting condemns its victim to perpetual motion. It is nothing but scratch, scratch, scratch all the time, till we are literally scarred from the process."

A tour of the immense block of buildings that constitute the Grey Nunnery of Montreal is an enterprise that severely taxes one's powers of walking and endurance. The wiry little nun who showed me round was evidently accustomed to the business, for she trotted upstairs and downstairs, and through a bewildering maze of courts, corridors, dormitories, playgrounds, and gardens, finishing up as fresh and lively as when she started. From my experience, I would recommend succeeding visitors to take this immense and versatile institution one frontage at a time. Trying to crowd the whole of it into a single visit means a long and toilsome tramp, followed by a mass of confused impressions. The Grey Nuns have a printing-press and book-binding establishment that turns out excellent work. Fancy cards, flowers, pictures, statues scapulars, and rosaries are all prepared by the skilful hands of the nuns; they have, also, a complete pharmacy and dentist's shop; they manufacture beautiful processional banners, altar decorations, and church vestments; they have a big boot-maker's shop, and a room near at hand where six nuns are hard at work with knitting machines; and as for the laundries, there seems to be room and appliances enough on the premises to take up a contract for the washing of Christendom. There are departments for babies, boys, girls, old men, and aged women; and so comprehensive is the establishment that visitors to Montreal who would rather stay in a convent than in an hotel or a boarding-house have here their wishes and requirements catered for in the most complete and satisfactory style. In the centre of the conventual block is the Church of the Holy Cross—a spacious, well-proportioned, and very pleasingly decorated edifice. It is almost needless to add that many thousands of dollars have to be expended every year by the Grey Sisters for the support of the numerous philanthropic, charitable, and educational institutions that are grouped together in this block. They have four sources of revenue, the rents of the houses and lands belonging to the community, a Government grant of 2200 dollars, the united industries of the establishment, and the donations of friends and visitors. "Servants of the Poor" is the motto of the Grey Nuns of Montreal, and right well do they act up to it.

IV.

IN THE CANADIAN CAPITAL.

AUSTRALIA presents some remarkable examples of the rapid creation of prosperous cities, but even the annals of the Antipodes will be searched in vain for a parallel to the rapidity with which the little village of Bytown has blossomed into the beautiful and busy city of Ottawa, the political metropolis of the Dominion of Canada. Occupying a most picturesque and favoured position at the junction of the Ottawa and Rideau Rivers, its progress in the past is only a foretaste of the prosperity and the expansion that the future has assuredly in store for it. Already Ottawa is a place of considerable commercial importance, a great centre of the lumber trade, the site of numerous saw-mills that turn out the huge piles of prepared timber which meet the eye at every turn. The founders of the Dominion, like the creators of the neighbouring Republic, prudently passed over their large and populous cities in choosing their future capital, and fixed upon a quiet little village on the border line between the two great provinces of Quebec and Ontario. That little village was the chrysalis from which the imposing and well-appointed city of Ottawa has been evolved. As befits the historical origin and distinctive character of this newest and brightest of cities, the buildings in which the legislative and administrative business of the Dominion of Canada is conducted are the first to arrest the eye of the visitor. They constitute a noble and imposing group, occupying a spacious and elevated square, from which the wide, tree-environed streets and long rows of substantially built shops and houses spread away on one side, while on the other the broad waterway of the Ottawa River, flanked by successive symmetrical mountains of sawn-up timber, is seen careering through a smiling, sunlit valley, dotted at intervals with farms and gardens. Constructed of a bright-looking, yellowish sort of stone, and arranged with marked architectural effect, the Government buildings tower aloft and dominate the scene from every point of view in Ottawa. The eastern and western wings comprise long ranges of Government offices, the central structure constituting the Parliamentary buildings proper. The chambers in which the Senate and the House of Commons meet are handsome, commodious, and well-lighted halls. There are no benches, as at Westminster, every Minister and member having his own appointed chair and writing-desk. This system is an obvious improvement on Westminster in several respects. Many an onlooker has sincerely sympathized with Mr. Gladstone and Mr. Balfour when these leaders of the House had, late in the evening, to write the report of the day's proceedings for the information of Her Majesty. The knees drawn uncomfortably close together, the blotting-pad carefully balanced upon them, the left hand fully employed in keeping the paper steady on the blotting-pad, while the right was either nervously propelling the pen or scooting around for a dip of ink, the whole arrangement being liable to be overwhelmed at any moment, and the manuscript irretrievably smudged by the passing coat-tails of a careless colleague—all this is a familiar spectacle at Westminster, and one that clearly calls for a reform of some sort. At the same time, to supply every Member at Westminster with a chair and a desk would necessitate the construction of a Chamber three or four times the size of the present one, and that in its turn would necessitate members speaking from a tribune in French fashion; and altogether the problem of satisfactorily seating the 670 representatives of the people at Westminster will take some years yet to solve. At the rear of the Ottawa Legislative Chambers is a bright, elegant, and capacious rotunda, containing 160,000 volumes, in every department of literature. Technically it is the Parliamentary Library, but practically it is open to the public and to every accredited visitor. It possesses a very valuable collection of pamphlets and documents bearing on the early history of Canada. The University of Ottawa—an extensive pile which is passed on the way to Rideau Hall, the official residence of the Governor-General—is one of the largest Catholic educational establishments of the Dominion. It has Faculties of Theology, Law, Philosophy, and Arts. The Geological and Natural History Museum in Sussex Street is an Ottawa institution in which a very agreeable and instructive afternoon may be spent. Here are preserved many mementoes of the Indian tribes of Canada—wampum belts, sacrificial stones, quaint head-dresses, etc.—while the mineral and vegetable productions of the Dominion are displayed with a profusion that severely taxes the exhibiting capacity of the building. The Curator of the Museum, and head of the Canadian Geological Department, is Dr. A. R. C. Selwyn, whose name is familiar to the scientific world of Great Britain. The son of a Canon of Gloucester Cathedral, he assisted in the geological survey of Great Britain in 1845, and seven years later the Secretary of State for the Colonies despatched him to Melbourne to supervise the geological survey of Victoria. There he remained, doing good work, until 1869, when he was called to Canada to succeed Sir W. E. Logan as chief of the Geological Department. Although now in his seventieth year, he is as vigorous and enthusiastic as ever in the furtherance of his favourite science.

Some amateur theologian has dogmatically declared that "there are only two live religions in the world—Catholicism and Methodism." Without endorsing such a sweeping assertion, or saying anything calculated to arouse the slumbering lion of religious controversy, it may be confessed, and will be generally admitted, that the Catholic and Methodist Churches are the most conspicuous in the public eye for untiring zeal, manifold activities, and completeness of ecclesiastical organization. Each retains a firm hold on its own adherents, and a wanderer from the camp of the one into the fold of the other is a very rare bird indeed. In the Catholic Church you will find many ex-Anglicans, ex-Presbyterians, and ex-Congregationalists, but an ex-Methodist is like the proverbial needle in the stack of hay. I have heard of them, but the Prime Minister of the Dominion of Canada is the first Catholic ex-Methodist with whom I have actually conversed.[1] Born in Halifax, the metropolis of Nova Scotia, half a century ago, Sir John

---

[1] This sketch of Sir John Thompson was written immediately after a very gracious and interesting interview with him in Ottawa. A few weeks afterwards I was greatly shocked and grieved to read in Australia a cable message announcing his sudden death at Windsor Castle while on a visit to Her Majesty.

Thompson was brought up, trained, and educated as a Methodist, and when, in his thirtieth year, he made up his mind to become a Catholic, he risked the loss of the large and lucrative legal practice that he had established amongst the Methodists of his native province. They were naturally greatly disturbed and mortified at the unexpected news, but to their credit be it recorded, there was nothing whatever in the nature of uncharitable reprisals, and Sir John did not lose a solitary client by his change of religion. Many people are drawn into the Catholic Church by the magnificence, the solemnity, and the picturesqueness of the ritual; some are captivated by the pulpit oratory, while others attach themselves to the Rock of Peter from the crying need of an infallible guide that they experience in their souls. But it was by none of these paths that Sir John Thompson entered the Catholic Church. A controversial book he happened to read set him thinking. He was irresistibly impelled into a minute and careful investigation of the whole subject; he approached the great problem from the standpoint of law and logic; he conscientiously and impartially applied the rules of evidence to existing creeds, and he finally arrived at the conclusion that the Catholic Church had the first and foremost claim on his spiritual allegiance, and was the Divinely-appointed bulwark of law, order, and authority in the world.

In the Canadian Capital.

Sir John Thompson is colloquially known in Canadian Parliamentary circles as "the little giant," because, though small in stature, he has a gigantic capacity for work. He resembles Lord Rosebery in the easy grace and the quiet affability of his manner; but behind these drawing-room accomplishments it is not difficult to discover the solid qualities of the statesman—the tact, the shrewdness, the skill in the management of men, the keen perception and the comprehensive grasp of the subject under discussion, and the well-studied success with which, by a single striking and significant phrase, he happily illuminates the whole arena of debate. In a word, Sir John Thompson impresses you as a born leader of men, with a considerable amount of reserve force in his composition. He was discovered by Sir John Macdonald, the chief founder and first Premier of Federated Canada, whom he has succeeded as Conservative Prime Minister of the Dominion. He learnt shorthand while studying for the Bar in Nova Scotia, and he finds the stenographic art very serviceable to him in the Dominion House of Commons, for it enables him to take down the vital parts of his opponents' speeches verbatim, to quote them with telling effect, and to pulverize them with a few rounds of his ready verbal artillery. After a successful career at the Nova Scotian Bar, he was appointed Attorney-General in 1878, subsequently assuming the Premiership of the Province as well, and resigning both offices in July, 1882, on his acceptance of a judgeship of the Supreme Court of Nova Scotia. Thirty-eight was a very early age to retire into the dignified obscurity of a judgeship, but he was not destined to rust on the Bench very long. Sir John Macdonald wanted a good debating Attorney-General in the Dominion House of Commons, and he soon made up his mind that Judge Thompson was the man to fill the situation. And so the young judge entered the Dominion House of Commons as senior law officer in the Ministry of Sir John Macdonald. The ascendancy he rapidly acquired in the counsels of the Canadian popular Chamber, by reason of his high personal character, his unwearying industry, his superabundant energy, and his acknowledged Parliamentary ability, is best evidenced by the unanimity with which, on the death of Sir John Macdonald, he was nominated to the succession of the Conservative leadership. For a time he displayed a strong disinclination to assume the onerous responsibility of the Premiership; but circumstances at length compelled him to bow to the inevitable, and he now seems perfectly at home in the Prime Minister's chair. He received his knighthood in recognition of the valuable services he rendered to the British representatives on the Fishery Commission at Washington in 1887.

In the Canadian Capital.

As the originator and the chairman of the Imperial Conference that recently deliberated at Ottawa, the name of Sir Mackenzie Bowell has become familiar to the British public. He will live in history as the organizer and the president of the first gathering of the statesmen of Greater Britain that has assembled in a Colonial metropolis. Sir Mackenzie Bowell thus narrated to me the circumstances that impelled him to suggest a Colonial Conference at Ottawa:—" As the result of Mr. Huddart's enterprise in starting a direct line of steamers between Australia and Canada, we discovered and realized great possibilities for the development and expansion of Canadian trade with the Australasian Colonies. Sir John Thompson advised that I should visit Australasia and confer with the various Governments there as to the best means of mutually developing trade between Canada and Australia. I went out to Australia, but soon after landing there I discovered that I had undertaken a bigger contract than I could possibly carry out within the limited time at my command. There was no federal authority with whom I could negotiate and exchange ideas. On the contrary, I found seven independent Governments, some with their Parliaments in full activity, others in recess. I met a number of leading Australian statesmen, and received from them every kindness, sympathy, and encouragement. But there was no getting away from the fact that I could not possibly cover the ground during my visit, and that to secure practical results a little formal deliberation would be better than any amount of informal interviews; and so I struck in boldly with the suggestion that we should have a regularly-organized Inter-Colonial Conference at Ottawa. The idea was taken up splendidly by all the Colonies, and it assumed dimensions that did not enter into my contemplation at the outset. But the Conference, as you know, was a remarkable success. It was attended by the most eminent statesmen of Australasia, the Cape, and Canada, and the delegate of the Imperial Government, Lord Jersey, gave us most valuable assistance by his experienced advice, and the promptings of his cautious Conservatism." "He acted as an Imperial brake on your Colonial precipitancy," I interposed. "Well, yes, something of that sort," Sir Mackenzie laughingly replied. Pending the publication of the official report of the proceedings of the Conference, he was precluded from entering into details, but he was satisfied that the Conference had done good work, and would have far-reaching results in the direction of Colonial cohesion and Imperial unity. Sir Mackenzie Bowell was born at Rickinghall, Suffolk, seventy-one years ago, but as a boy of ten he was brought by his parents from England to Canada. He took to journalism when he grew up to man's estate, became editor and proprietor of a couple of Canadian papers, and was elected to the Presidency of the Ontario Press Association. He has been in the Dominion Parliament since 1867, and Sir John Macdonald made him Minister of Trade and Customs in 1878. From 1870 until 1878 he was the "Most Worshipful Grand Master and Sovereign of the Orange Association of British America."

The fact that Orangemen and Irish Catholics get along very comfortably and harmoniously together in Canada was brought under my notice by Sir Mackenzie Bowell himself, who emphasized his long and intimate friendship with his Ministerial colleague, Mr. Curran, Solicitor-General, as a case in point. As a further illustration, it is worthy of note that the Dominion Ministry brings into brotherly embrace the Hon. N. C. Wallace, the present Grand Master of the Orangemen of British America, and the Hon. John Costigan, an ardent Irish Nationalist, and the mover of the Address to the Queen from the Dominion Parliament in 1882, praying her Majesty to grant Home Rule to Ireland. The fact is, that when Orangemen and Nationalists find themselves standing shoulder to shoulder in the work of building up a great Dominion, they naturally, and almost of necessity, learn to be tolerant and conciliatory towards each other, while adhering to their respective opinions on the subjects of Ireland and the Pope. The root of the

"Ulster difficulty" is to be found in the fact that the Orangemen and Nationalists of Ireland have little or no opportunity of standing shoulder to shoulder for the promotion of the prosperity of their common country. Mr. Curran, who has been the Conservative Member for Central Montreal for a dozen years, is one of the principal chiefs of the Canadian Irish Nationalists, and has done much by his voice, pen, and purse to promote the Home Rule cause. He is an excellent platform speaker, and a lawyer of the highest repute. Frank, genial, courteous, and hospitable, Mr. Curran is an admirable type of the successful Irish colonist. He is widely popular with all parties and creeds in Canada.

V.

THE QUEEN CITY.

Toronto, which is colloquially known by this superior and somewhat ambitious title, avowedly aspires to supremacy amongst the cities of Canada, and bids fair to realize her hopes at no distant date. She is rapidly overtaking Montreal in size and population. At present the latter has fifty thousand people to the good; but if Toronto continues its recent rate of progress the next census returns will probably show that the Queen City has forged ahead of its rival in the race for the civic premiership. Splendidly situated on the northern shore of Lake Ontario, and served alike by the New York and St. Lawrence routes, the commercial possibilities of Toronto are so vast and varied that not much prophetic insight is needed for the prediction that it is destined to become the Canadian Chicago. Already it is a wonderful city, palpitating with life and energy, full of colossal business establishments, and presenting all the evidences of abounding material prosperity in the present, and the promise of far greater progress in the future. Both as regards race and religion, Toronto is the antithesis of Montreal. The latter is mainly peopled by the French and the Irish, and Catholicism is everywhere in the ascendant, whereas in Toronto, the English and the Scotch constitute the great majority, and Protestantism is the prevailing creed. Toronto is a Mohawk Indian word, signifying "a place of meeting," and, as a French trading post, a good many business meetings with the Indians were held there during the eighteenth century. When General Simcoe entered into possession for the British, in 1794, he christened it York, and York it remained until 1834, when, on being incorporated, it resumed its old Indian name. Its population then was less than ten thousand; now it rejoices in a quarter of a million. The Torontonians are fully conscious of the supreme excellence of themselves and their city, and they are not disposed to be taciturn on the subject. In the introduction to the current issue of their official City Directory a pretty lofty note of adulation in honour of "our noble selves" is sounded:—"There is no doubt Toronto is the finest city on the continent for its size. Our citizens generally are more respectable in appearance; our laws are better observed and more strictly enforced; we have more beautiful residence streets, with substantial and comfortable homes surrounded by fine lawns, ornamental shrubs, and shady trees; we have more handsome and healthy-looking ladies; and our female clerks, stenographers, factory girls, etc., have a finer appearance than those of any other city." There is a good deal of truth in these allegations, but they would come with more grace and conviction from the impartial and admiring stranger within the gates. From the letters of that distinguished citizen of Toronto, Professor Goldwin Smith, to the *Times*, and from the fact that Toronto has very intimate and important commercial relations with the great republic on the other side of the lakes, I expected to find an appreciable current of opinion in favour of annexation to the United States; but careful and extensive inquiries led to the conclusion that the pro-annexation movement has little or no depth, significance, or substantial influence in Toronto.

Toronto possesses one of the finest and best-appointed public libraries and reading-rooms in the British Empire. The staff is composed of bright and intelligent young ladies, who do their work with a smartness and precision that pointedly indicate this as a peculiarly appropriate sphere of feminine usefulness. The establishment is a very extensive one, embracing a circulating library of eighty-five thousand volumes, to which constant additions of the newest literature are being made; a large newspaper-room, displaying the latest journals from Great Britain and all the leading Colonies; a separate reading-room for ladies, and a reference library of a most complete and up-to-date description. Furthermore, branches have been opened in different parts of the city, and the people of Toronto have certainly every reason to congratulate themselves on the exceptional facilities for literary culture and recreation that they enjoy. These facilities are evidently appreciated and turned to the best account. The central institution, brilliantly illuminated with the electric light, is crowded every evening with earnest, thoughtful, well-conducted students and readers, while the ladies in charge of the circulating library are kept busy throughout the day receiving and exchanging books.

Toronto, as the capital of the province of Ontario, is the residence of a Lieutenant-Governor, and the meeting-place of a provincial legislature. Colonel Kirkpatrick, the present local Governor, is a native Canadian of Irish parentage, a silver medallist of Trinity College, Dublin, and was one of the Canadian Commissioners to the Indian and Colonial Exhibition, held at South Kensington in 1886. Sir Oliver Mowatt, the Premier and Attorney-General of the province, is a veteran of seventy-four, of Scottish descent, and was a fellow-student of the law with Sir John Macdonald. He has been a barrister since 1841, and a Q.C. since 1856. For twenty-two years he was the President of the

Evangelical Alliance of Ontario. Sir Frank Smith, a member of the Dominion Senate, and one of the most prominent figures in the commercial life of Toronto, is a native of Armagh, Ireland, and is now in his seventy-second year. His name is associated with almost all the business activities and joint-stock enterprises that have been instrumental in building up the commercial greatness of Canada's "Queen City." An eminent citizen and public man of Toronto has since 1892 figured on the larger and more conspicuous stage of Westminster, in the person of the Hon. Edward Blake, who shares with Mr. Justin M'Carthy the representation of the county of Longford in the Imperial Parliament. Mr. Blake's election to a seat in the House of Commons has by no means terminated his active connection with Canadian affairs. He still retains the Chancellorship of the University of Toronto, and a large share in a local long-established legal business. Mr. Blake, who was for some time Premier of the province of Ontario, holds that the future of Canada is largely dependent on the development of the great North-West Territory. He is also of opinion that the present form of connection between the Mother Country and Canada does not possess the element of permanence. As the child grows into the man, so, he says, the State will come to maturity, and notwithstanding the enormous difficulties that surround the ideal of Imperial

Federation, he believes there is a possibility and a hope of reorganizing the Empire on a Federal basis, so as to reconcile British connection with British freedom.

VI.

THE METROPOLIS OF MANITOBA.

FORT WILLIAM, on the western shore of Lake Superior, which is reached after a couple of days' delightful steaming over the great inland seas of North America, is not now the handful of huts that it was in 1870, when Colonel (now Lord) Wolseley assembled his army here to march to the Red River, and suppress the rebellion of the half-breeds under Louis Riel. It has grown into a thriving, progressive town of between three and four thousand inhabitants, with numerous hotels and shops, several churches, a couple of newspapers, and a town-hall. One of its journals is called the *Echo*, and I was somewhat amused at the conditions under which this Canadian copy of the Catherine Street original was produced. It was edited, printed, and published in the upper storey of a plain weather-board building, whose lower half was occupied as a Chinese laundry, three industrious Mongolians being visible through the open doors and uncurtained windows, hard at work on shirts and collars, while seated at a window overhead was a severe-looking gentleman, plying a pen with vigour, and seemingly determined to correct some crying local grievance or die in the attempt. And this is a reminder of a fact that I noticed in nearly all the Canadian cities and towns, the extent to which the Chinese are rapidly monopolizing the laundry business. In Montreal, Toronto, and other places, you come across Chinese laundries in almost every street you traverse, and before long the Mongolian will capture the clothes-washing industry as completely in Canada as he has already done in the United States. From Fort William—which was literally a fort in the old days when it was a fur-trading post of the Hudson's Bay Company, and when the Indians around were fond of white men's scalps—to Winnipeg, the metropolis of the province of Manitoba, the railway line runs within view of tumbling rivers, peaceful lakes, thickly-timbered ranges, the beginnings of townships, periodical clearings, where pioneer farmers have commenced cultivation, saw-mills on a gigantic scale, and, as Winnipeg is approached, a succession of smiling farms and embryonic cities. Winnipeg is another striking example of the rapidity with which favourable conditions will transform a little insignificant hamlet into a populous and prosperous metropolitan city. When Lord Wolseley arrived at Fort Garry, as it was then called, in 1870, the population was only 200. Ten years afterwards it had mounted up to 6500, last year it was 30,000, and to-day it is over 35,000, with every indication that the increase will be similarly continuous in the future. As I write these words I can see from the window of my Winnipeg hotel new streets in process of formation at various points, and new houses going up in all directions. My eye wanders over a compact, well-built, bustling city, with wide, tree-bordered streets, through which electric cars are perpetually careering; lofty business houses and extensive factories, church spires, and handsome public edifices. Situated at the junction of the Red River with the Assiniboine, the advantages of the site for trading purposes were realized and utilized at an early period of the white occupation of British North America, but it was not until the rich agricultural lands of Manitoba and the North-West Territories were taken up and occupied, that Fort Garry began its rushing career of progress and prosperity, and developed into the now famous and flourishing city of Winnipeg. The secret of Winnipeg's rapid rise and constantly-growing greatness is to be found in the fact that, by reason of its unique geographical position, it is the receiving depôt and the distributing centre for nearly the whole of Manitoba and the North-West. The settlement of these vast and fertile territories involved almost of necessity a great and brilliant future for Winnipeg. As the

Marquis of Lorne very truly and felicitously characterized it, Winnipeg is "the heart city of the Dominion," adding that "nowhere can you find a situation whose natural advantages promise so great a future." Railways converge on Winnipeg from all points of the compass, and thousands of miles of river navigation supplement the resources of the rail, and contribute largely to the volume of business transacted daily in the Manitoban metropolis. The Canadian Pacific Railway Company have extensive workshops here, and a considerable amount of labour is employed in the numerous manufactories of all the machines and implements requisite for the large and growing farming population of Manitoba and the North-West.

In addition to its commercial pre-eminence, Winnipeg is politically important as the residence of the Lieutenant-Governor and the seat of the Manitoba Legislature. The Parliamentary buildings constitute a handsome and commodious whitish brick pile on Broadway. As at Ottawa, they embrace an excellent library and reading-room. In the latter I was pleased to see files of all the leading Australian newspapers, showing the intimate relations that have been developed between Canada and Australasia by the new direct steam service connecting Vancouver and Sydney. On the block adjoining the Parliamentary buildings stands the official residence of the Lieutenant-

Governor, a handsome and bright-looking brick mansion, with a cannon on the lawn and a Union Jack flying from the tower as outward and visible symbols of lawful delegated authority. To judge from his name alone, Governor John Christian Schultz would perhaps not be regarded at first sight as a British subject. But he is, nevertheless, a native Canadian, born in Essex, Ontario, fifty-four years ago. His foreign name is accounted for by the fact that his father was a Norwegian, who married an Irish lady, Miss Elizabeth Riley, of Bandon, County Cork. Governor Schultz is a medical man by profession and a scientist by inclination. In the latter character he came to Fort Garry in 1860, collecting botanical specimens, so he ranks among the living pioneers and veterans of Winnipeg. Deciding to settle down in the district, he took an active and prominent part both in its commercial and educational development. He was a powerful and conspicuous advocate of the confederation of the Canadian provinces, and when the North-West was added to the Dominion, in 1869, he became the special target for the hostility of the disaffected elements of the population. The latter attacked and captured Fort Garry ; he stood a siege for some time in his own house, but when all supplies were cut off by the insurgents, he and his garrison of thirty-nine were taken prisoners. After two months of imprisonment he managed to escape, and notwithstanding that a reward was offered for his capture, dead or alive, and all the ordinary routes were vigilantly guarded by the insurgents, he succeeded, although with much toil, danger, and difficulty, in making his way to Ottawa. When matters had quieted down and Manitoba became a regularly organized province of the Dominion, he was returned at the first General Election to the Dominion House of Commons, and held his seat until 1882, when he was raised to the Senate. He has been the Lieutenant-Governor of Manitoba since 1888. The Premier of the Province, the Hon. Thomas Greenway, is a native of Cornwall, and came to Canada just half a century ago, when he was a boy of six. He is not such an aggressive-looking Cornishman as the Right Hon. Leonard Courtney, but the solid common-sense and unwavering determination that are conspicuous elements of the Cornish character reveal themselves in the conversation and career of Mr. Greenway. He has been actively associated with Canadian politics since 1875, and his Premiership of the Province of Manitoba dates from January, 1888. His hands are pretty full, for he is not only Premier, but President of the Council, Minister of Agriculture and Immigration, and Commissioner of Railways to boot. Mr. Greenway comes of a colonizing family. He has near relatives in Melbourne, and he informed me that he intends embracing the earliest opportunity to run across the Pacific and see them. Formerly it was a matter of considerable delay and difficulty for a Canadian to visit his Australian cousins, but now, thanks to the enterprising Mr. Huddart, who has built a bridge between the two dominions, the trip can be accomplished at an almost inappreciable loss of time and money.

VII.

THE PRAIRIE PROVINCE.

No portion of the British Dominions during recent years has been more conspicuously connected with emigration from the Old World than Manitoba. The "Prairie Province," in point of fact, has become a sort of synonym for "the land to emigrate to." When Mr. John Morley, in Opposition, described the Irish policy of Lord Salisbury and Mr. Balfour as one of "Manacles or Manitoba," everybody recognized at once that he meant to suggest that the Conservatives were placing two extreme alternatives before the Irish people—either stay at home and submit to coercion, or clear out to the "Prairie Province." The Irish settlers in Manitoba are fairly numerous, but the population of the province, as a whole, is best indicated by the word cosmopolitan. All the peoples and nationalities of Europe and America are represented in this fertile and progressive province of the Canadian Dominion. The reason of this rush from every country in the world to Manitoba is not far to seek. Here was an immense area of the richest agricultural land in existence, presenting no pioneering difficulties whatever, but ready for occupation and cultivation the moment the settler arrived in any part of it. When one remembers the tremendous up-hill difficulties that pioneer settlers have had to resolutely face and wearily conquer in other portions of the British Empire—the clearing away of encumbering forests, the perils of fire and flood, the privations of solitude, and the constant fear of attacks from savages—there is no occasion for surprise that these millions of fertile acres of treeless prairies, bisected by the Canadian Pacific Railway and within easy reach of both the Atlantic and the Pacific seaboards, should have been rushed by people from every clime. The dimensions of this rush may be gauged from the fact that while the last Canadian census showed that the population of the Dominion, as a whole, had increased by 11 per cent., that of the Province of Manitoba alone had increased by no less than 148 per cent. But this progress, marvellous as it is, does not satisfy the Manitoban Premier. When I expressed my astonishment at such a rapid rate of increase, Mr. Greenway assured me that he was somewhat disappointed that the population did not come much faster. And, no doubt, if people generally knew as well as Mr. Greenway knows the immense amount of wealth that lies on the surface of the soil of Manitoba, and the unprecedented ease with which that wealth can be garnered and stored, the Prairie Province, big as it is, would very soon be filled up from end to end. The Premier is a successful Manitoba farmer himself, and he wonders why Old World farmers should be perpetually complaining that they cannot make agriculture pay, when they have only got to move to Manitoba and share the prosperity of the most prosperous agricultural community on the face of the globe. A score of expert witnesses have borne high testimony to the agricultural capabilities of the Prairie Province. For instance, Professor Tanner, of the Department of Agriculture, South Kensington, does not hesitate to say that "in Manitoba are to be found the champion soils of the world, and we may rejoice that they are located within the British Empire." There are several colonies of Scotch crofters in Manitoba, and they are all now thoroughly settled down and doing well. Scandinavians and Germans have also established themselves in Manitoba in considerable numbers, and I was officially assured that they make excellent colonists. A significant feature is the large influx from the neighbouring republic. When Manitoba first commenced to attract attention as an eminently advantageous field for emigration, the Americans were exceedingly sceptical, and even openly depreciatory, but now they have changed their tune, and are crossing the border to the new land of promise in thousands.

The visits of the farmers' delegates from Great Britain and Ireland, and the laudatory character of their reports, have done much to stimulate emigration from the British Isles to Manitoba. As a typical sample of these reports, that of Mr. Robert Pitt, Ilminster, may be cited:—"I have endeavoured to describe the state of things in Manitoba and the North-West, which is undoubtedly the country for an English labourer to go to. If he has but 8l. or 9l. he can pay his passage, and, by arriving out there at seeding or harvest-time, he can be assured of work from that moment at a figure which will vary according to his competence; and if he will only keep himself to himself, and keep his eyes about him, he is safe to be a landlord in three years, and an established man for life." Rarely, if ever, has Hodge had such a rosy prospect as that brought within the purview of his possibilities. A very appreciable element of the English emigration to Manitoba consists of young fellows who come out with a hazy idea of becoming gentleman-farmers. A number of them do settle on the land and prosper, but, as might have been expected, a proportion of them soon get tired of the uncongenial life, and drift into the cities and towns. I was informed that many of the clerks and shop assistants in Winnipeg belonged to this class. Dr. Barnardo has made Manitoba the theatre of his philanthropic and reforming experiments with the street boys of London and other large English cities. At Russell, some forty miles to the north of Winnipeg, he has established a large farm and agricultural training-school. Here the lads are received and put through a regular course of practical agricultural education. When they are deemed proficient in all that pertains to agricultural operations, they are drafted out to farmers who have applied for their services. It is yet too early to say whether good permanent colonists can or will be developed out of such unpromising material as the waifs and strays of the London streets. The local testimony on the subject is conflicting. Whilst the officials who have special supervision of land settlement in Manitoba declare that the "Barnardo boys" (the phrase in common use in the Prairie Province) get on well, and give satisfaction as a body, unofficial observers shake their heads, and allege that many of the youngsters relapse and drift away into space, unreformed, and apparently uninfluenced for the better, by the Barnardo course of moral treatment. Some of the Canadian newspapers, I notice, are endeavouring to put a stop to the immigration of "Barnardo boys," not on the ground that the lads are failures or morally undesirable, but because Canada has enough boys of her own to meet the requirements of her farms.

The Canadian Pacific Railway Company is one of the most extensive agents for the promotion of

British settlement in Manitoba. As part payment for the construction of the iron road from the Atlantic to the Pacific, the company owns some twenty-five millions of acres in alternate blocks abutting on the track. These peculiarly-favoured areas are being largely taken up, and it will not be long before the steam-engine will run right through Manitoba without ever losing sight of a farm or a homestead. At Winnipeg the company has a large land office in connection with its railway station, and it would be hard to say which of the two departments was the busier.

After running for hours and hours along the level but luxuriant expanse of the Prairie Province, the railway enters the great North-Western region, where ranching, or sheep and cattle raising, is the principal pursuit. Not that farming ceases when Manitoba is left behind. On the contrary, the farmers are pushing their way beyond the Manitoban boundary and picking out the farming areas in close proximity to the railway. Lord Brassey, for instance, has established two splendid farms near the Indian Head Station, one of them bearing the title of his famous yacht, the *Sunbeam*. Still farther West, the Earl of Aberdeen, before he became Governor-General of Canada, entered into business as a fruit cultivator on a colossal scale, and he still continues the industry by deputy, most of his time being now necessarily passed in the metropolis of the Dominion. Law and order in the North-West are maintained by the mounted police, a splendid body, a thousand strong, largely composed of young Englishmen. They wear a striking military uniform, and have an unmistakably soldier-like bearing and aspect. Their headquarters is at Regina, a rising city of 3000 inhabitants, the residence of the Lieutenant-Governor, and the meeting-place of the legislative body of the North-West Territories. In this little Parliament of twenty-two members, an Irish peer, then known as Viscount Boyle, sat as member for Macleod. There are more scions of nobility and young Britons of good family leading a free, airy, open, healthy, and romantic life on the ranches of the North-West Territories—a sort of high-class corps of amateur cowboys—than in any other quarter of Greater Britain.

VIII.

OVER THE ROCKIES.

From Regina to Calgary, a stretch of about 500 miles, the Canadian Pacific Railway runs through a splendid ranching country, great heaps of buffaloes' skulls and skeletons, visible at intervals from the carriage windows, telling of the success and completeness with which the great animal monarch of North America has been practically exterminated in order to make room for horses, sheep, and cattle. The ranches continue in almost unbroken succession right up to the base of the Rocky Mountains, covering the foothills, and occupying the intervening valleys. The scriptural allusion to cattle grazing on a thousand hills is at once recalled to the memory and realized with literal accuracy as the train commences its long and arduous climb to the summit of the great dividing range. At Calgary, a handsome and go-ahead town of 5000 inhabitants, called into being by the requirements of the numerous ranches for hundreds of miles around, the ascent of the Rockies may be said to begin, although their snow-clad **peaks** and serrated lines, stretching away **as far** as the eye can travel along the southern and western horizon, are by no means so close at hand as they look. The iron horse has to puff and pant for several hours yet before the Rockies are strictly and actually reached. Another engine is there in readiness to assist the train up the steepest sections of the formidable series of mountain barriers that seem to set all engineering skill and science at defiance. But here, as elsewhere, man has proved himself more than a match for the most Titanic forces of **Nature**. Tremendous **yawning** abysses have been successfully bridged, **pathways** for the passage of the locomotive have been hewn and blasted out of the sides of appalling precipices; long, narrow, and sinuous gorges, environed by walls that **shoot** up straight **for** hundreds, and in some places thousands, of feet, **have** been compelled to pay a sufficient tribute of territory to the conquering engineer; and the host of obstacles thrown in the way of his advance by rushing rivers, foaming cataracts, snow, ice, and colossal rocks have been overcome and removed by patience, perseverance, and scientific ingenuity. The scenery throughout these 500 miles of mountain locomotion is indescribably grand and impressive—snow-clad ranges, sun-illumined glaciers, beautifully-wooded mountain-sides, awe-inspiring cañons, fantastically-shaped peaks, raging torrents, and charming cascades succeeding each other in panoramic variety and interest. To enable the passengers to enjoy this glorious scenic banquet to the full, an "observation car," or carriage open on all sides, is attached to the train, and affords facilities for an unobstructed and satisfying view. The stations in this Alpine region represent either spots of special attractiveness, where hotels have been erected for the accommodation of excursionists, or mining townships that have sprung up in the vicinity of gold, silver, or coal deposits, for the Rocky Mountains constitute a rich and still largely undeveloped mineral region, as well as a theatre of unsurpassable scenic wonders and delights.

The province of the Canadian Dominion that lies between the Rocky Mountains and the Pacific may claim the credit of having practically called the great Trans-continental railway into existence, for British Columbia, before agreeing to join the Canadian Confederation, stipulated that a railway should be constructed to connect her with the Eastern Provinces, and, furthermore, that it should be commenced within two years from the date of joining the Dominion. Sir John Macdonald (the father of the Federation) persuaded the first Parliament of the Dominion to agree to these terms, although the proposal was strenuously opposed by the Liberals, who contended that the projected line had never been properly surveyed, and that the cost of its construction would tie a tremendous mill-stone of debt around the neck of the infant Dominion. Sir John, having carried a Bill to provide for the construction of the railway, dissolved the House, and appealed to the country to ratify his policy in the matter. The country endorsed his action, strengthened his hands, and solidified the growing federation. Thus the Canadian Pacific Railway was started into being—a permanent bond of union between the scattered provinces of the Dominion, as well as a monumental piece of successful engineering—in the teeth of the most formidable and terrific of natural difficulties. British Columbia did good business for itself, as well as the Dominion, in stipulating for the construction of the railway as an indispensable condition to its entering the Union. By the Rocky Mountains barrier it was practically isolated from the rest of British America, and the avenues for trade and commerce open to it in other directions were not particularly promising. The Canadian Pacific Railway has not only brought it into close and regular communication with the Eastern Provinces, but has enabled it to establish a very profitable connection with China, Japan, and Australia. The large and prosperous city of Vancouver has been created by the railway. It is the western terminus of the line, and from its capacious and picturesque harbour luxurious steamers are now regularly plying to Chinese, Japanese, and

Australian ports. Walking through the streets of this extensive city, bordered with long rows of well-appointed shops and business houses, with suburbs full of charming residences, and electric railway cars racing through all the leading thoroughfares, it is very difficult to realize that a few years ago the whole site was covered with a dense forest. Victoria, at the southern extremity of Vancouver Island, is the political capital of British Columbia, and also a place of considerable trade. It is a much more compact and English-looking city than Vancouver, but the latter has a much superior commercial position, and is obviously destined to rival San Francisco, and to develop into the most important British centre on the American side of the Pacific. There is a large Chinese quarter in Victoria, and the Mongolians appear to have captured a considerable amount of the business of the place. At Vancouver I noticed a number of shops displaying announcements that Chinese were not employed on the premises, and were in no way concerned in the business, a straw significant of an effort to divert public opinion into a channel hostile to the continued employment of the "heathen Chinee." But nothing short of a prohibitory poll-tax will keep Chinamen out of British Colonies. Once they get there, the amazing adaptability of their race, the readiness with which they pick up trades, their rigidly economical mode of life, their capacity for living and sleeping in the smallest possible space, and their freedom from domestic ties and responsibilities, give them an immense and unique advantage over all other competitors in the various fields of labour and industry. In addition to Vancouver and Victoria, British Columbia possesses a third important centre in New Westminster, whose inhabitants plume themselves on the fact that the title of their city was specially selected by Her Majesty the Queen.

When I arrived in British Columbia, I found the leader of the Liberal Party in the Dominion House of Commons, the Hon. Wilfred Laurier, engaged on a political speaking tour through the principal towns of the West, a rally being deemed advisable in view of the approach of a General Election. The Liberals have not been in power in Canada since 1878, and they naturally think it is about time for their long period of banishment from the Treasury benches to come to an end. Sixteen years' exclusion from office is the penalty they have had to pay for their uncompromising adherence to the principles and policy of Free Trade. Some bye-elections they have recently won have encouraged them in the hope that the ardour of Canadian devotion to Protection—the "national policy" adopted and legalized by Sir John Macdonald and the Conservatives—is beginning to cool. Free Trade has been the key-note of all Mr. Laurier's speeches in the

West. Canada he compares to a young giant shackled with the fetters of empirical economists. If the Liberals are returned to power at the coming General Election, he says they will " cut off the head of Protection and trample on its body." Mr. Laurier has made the most of the recent victory of Free Trade in New South Wales, and he exhorts the Canadians to go and do likewise when the opportunity arrives. From the enthusiasm with which he has been everywhere greeted in the West, the large crowds that have thronged to hear him, and the small majorities by which a number of the Protectionists were elected last time, it is evident that the creed of Cobden and Bright has far more adherents in Canada than the present state of parties at Ottawa would lead one to suppose. Mr. Laurier is a gentleman of fine presence, the pink of graceful courtesy and easy affability, and a platform orator of considerable power and eloquence. Although of French ancestry, he speaks English with unexceptionable purity and remarkable fluency. He is a descendant of one of the first families that colonized New France, as Canada was originally designated. In 1865, when he was in his twenty-fourth year, Mr. Laurier was called to the Canadian Bar, and he graduated as a Q.C. in 1880. He has been a member of the Dominion House of Commons continuously for twenty years, and is accounted one of the ablest debaters of Greater Britain.

IX.

THE NEWEST REPUBLIC.

From Vancouver to Honolulu, the metropolis of the newly-proclaimed Republic of Hawaii, is a very pleasant seven days' steaming excursion over the deep blue waters of the Pacific. The R.M.S. *Warrimoo* was patronized by a full complement of passengers this trip. There were Australians returning home by the "New Imperial Highway"; Canadians availing themselves of the facilities now afforded them to visit Australia, either for business or pleasure—mostly with the former intent; and a pretty considerable contingent of residents of Honolulu, getting back from the United States and Canada. These latter had a good deal to say about the latest revolution and the deposition of the dusky Queen of Hawaii. We invariably associate the word revolution in our minds either with the hurried flight of kings and queens or with their capture and decapitation on the scaffold. But there is nothing of that tragic description in the late revolutionary episode at Honolulu. The Queen of Hawaii was simply told by a committee of leading citizens that the monarchy was doomed, and that she must therefore be good enough to consider herself erased from the current list of reigning sovereigns. She naturally protested with womanly vehemence and indignation against such a sudden regal extinction, but with admirable tact, prudence, and common sense, she made no prolonged or exasperating fuss about the business; she bowed to the inevitable, retired from the palace before superior force, and took up her residence in a private house not far distant, where she is awaiting the next turn of the wheel of fortune, and where she will be ready to re-ascend the throne as soon as the fickle populace get tired of the Republic.[1] She has two of the Honolulu papers on her side; the native Hawaiians, who constitute the vast majority of the population, are understood, in a general sort of way, to be her sympathizers and adherents, but are apparently too lazy and unintelligent to organize and strike on her behalf; and there is, moreover, an influential section of English and American settlers, who took no part in the revolution, who disapprove of the change of government, and who are collectively referred to in the newspapers as the "Royalist Party." On the efforts

[1] Shortly after this was written, a Royalist restoration was attempted, but it proved a failure. The ex-Queen was arrested, tried by court-martial, and sentenced to five years' imprisonment.

and influence of this body, combined with the friendly intervention of the President of the United States, the ex-Queen's hopes of early restoration are founded. President Cleveland did, in point of fact, decree her restoration, but when he found that the execution of his mandate would meet with armed resistance, he unceremoniously backed out, and ungallantly left the lady in the lurch. As one of the Honolulu passengers on board the *Warrimoo* succinctly put it, in conversation with me, President Cleveland "miserably messed the business." There were quite a number of theories amongst the passengers as to the generating causes of the revolution. Some alleged that the determination of the Queen to make Honolulu a Pacific Monte Carlo was the source of her downfall; others ascribed the trouble to the Queen's systematically ignoring her responsible advisers, and allowing herself to be made the puppet of an objectionable clique; while a third group would have it that the Queen was conspiring to undermine the Constitution of the realm. A Yankee passenger opined that "they got up the revolution just for the fun of the thing," and possibly his guess may not be so wide of the mark as it looks. However that may be, certain it is that on the fourth of July (was it by accident or design that appropriate date was hit upon?) the Republic of Hawaii was formally and officially proclaimed at Honolulu. At the time of our arrival, towards the close of September, the oath of allegiance to the new Republic was being administered to the servants of the State, and officials of Royalist proclivities who declined to take it were being summarily dispensed with. The *Hawaiian Star*, the leading organ of the revolutionists, was writing very strongly on the subject: —" It is not to be supposed for a moment that the men and the political forces at the back of the Republic of Hawaii are playing make-believe in the establishment of a new form of Government, in which, perhaps, their lives, and certainly the majority of the financial interests of their countrymen, are concerned. The oath which is required as a pre-requisite for citizenship under the Republic is a fact representing individual responsibility under new conditions. It means that each individual taking it becomes a supporter and defender of a political reality, in place of an impracticable political theory." The new Republican Constitution provides that all male citizens twenty years of age who can fluently speak, read, and write either the English or the Hawaiian languages, are qualified to vote for the House of Representatives; that all lotteries and the sale of lottery tickets are prohibited; and that after the beginning of 1896 no public moneys be devoted to the support of any sectarian, denominational, or private school, or any school not under the exclusive control of the Government. But the most significant provision of the Constitution is this:—"The President, with the approval of the Cabinet, is hereby expressly authorized and empowered to make a treaty of political or commercial union between the Republic of Hawaii and the United States of America, subject to the ratification of the Senate." From this clause it is obvious that the Republic is only regarded as a temporary arrangement, and that the revolutionists look forward to annexation to the United States as soon as a more sympathetic president than Mr. Cleveland comes into power. The Americans constitute the bulk of the white population, but there is also a respectable colony of British settlers, and a considerable Portuguese element. Chinese and Japanese are also numerous, and are found very serviceable on the sugar plantations.

The metropolis of Hawaii is one of the most charmingly-situated cities on the face of the earth. Embowered in all the luxuriance of tropical foliage right down to the water's edge, and backed in the immediate distance by a lofty and precipitous mountain range, it presents to the admiring eyes on the approaching steamer the aspect of a carefully-protected garden of delights. Such is the wealth and all-pervadingness of tropical vegetation that most of the town is shut out from the view, although quite close at hand. The wharf at which our steamer was moored was thronged from end to end, the arrival of the mail steamer being the great event of the week. It was a cosmopolitan crowd, thoroughly representative of the various nationalities that have emigrated to the group on which the greatest of English navigators and discoverers, Captain Cook, lost his life. For the quarter of an hour that elapsed before our steamer was snugly placed in her appointed berth, she was surrounded by scores of active brown-skinned Hawaiian boys, all expert swimmers and divers, who secured the silver coins thrown from the deck long before the money had a chance of touching bottom. Going ashore, I soon perceived considerable improvements in Honolulu since I was last there in 1887. The streets were then villainously paved. They are not yet all that could be desired, but the principal thoroughfares are now very pleasing and satisfactory to pedestrians. The tramcar service is also an efficient reform, and I noticed that the buildings in the commercial quarter of the city were much larger and more substantial-looking than on the occasion of my former visit. H.M.S. *Hyacinth* was lying at anchor a hundred yards from the shore—a visible reminder to all concerned that British interests would not be allowed to suffer or British lives and property to be endangered by the quarrels of Royalists and Republicans. Several of the British residents with whom I conversed expressed the hope and the belief that if any annexation was to be done, England ought to do it, but, having regard to the fuss and outcry raised over the occupation of **Egypt, Uganda,** etc., I had to make the discouraging reply that, in my opinion, no British Government would feel disposed to take up another embarrassing contract of the like character in the North Pacific. The **Australian** Governments are very angry with **the new Hawaiian Republic for taking** formal possession of **Necker Island,** which had been designated as a desirable station on the route of the proposed British Pacific cable. They have energetically protested, but there is no use crying over spilt milk. Apart from the fact that Necker Island has always been regarded as within the Hawaiian sphere of influence, the representatives of the new Republic were undoubtedly the first to perform the ceremony of annexation. It was an indiscretion on the part of the Ottawa Conference to allow it to transpire that they contemplated Necker Island as a factor in the construction of the all-through British cable across the Pacific, before they had formally converted Necker Island into British soil. That the Hawaiian Government should have promptly taken advantage of this indiscretion is only natural, and what might reasonably have been expected under the circumstances. As the *Hawaiian Star* observes:—"The Australian Governments were preparing to take advantage of the fact that Hawaii had never taken possession of

Necker Island, and it had already been proposed at the Canadian Conference that Hawaii should be cut out of the proposed cable route by emphasizing the point that a Pacific cable should only touch at British territory, and, at the same time, including Necker Island as one of the proposed routes. To have refused to take formal possession of Necker Island, under the circumstances, would have been for the Republic to have shut its eyes to Hawaiian interests." There can be no doubt that the young Republic has scored a point in this business. When the work of constructing the Pacific cable is seriously taken in hand, Great Britain, Canada, and Australia must either purchase Necker Island outright, or compromise the situation by conceding a branch line from Necker Island to Honolulu.

X.

A CROWN COLONY.

SEVEN days after the infant Republic of Hawaii had vanished from our view, we steamed between long lines of coral reef into the harbour of Suva, the metropolis of the Crown Colony of Fiji. Suva, without possessing the mountainous background that sets off Honolulu to picturesque advantage, is remarkably prepossessing in its aspect when surveyed from the centre of the harbour. The town is literally embosomed in verdure, coming right down to the water's edge, and it gives obvious indications of future expansion over the hills that environ the harbour on every side. No sooner had we anchored than we were surrounded with boats manned by the brown-skinned natives of Fiji. These boats were filled with bunches of bananas and boxes of pineapples, and for the greater part of the day the Fijians, clad in the abbreviated costume of the *sulu*, or loin-cloth, were busily and vociferously engaged in transferring these pleasant and palatable fruits from their boats to our steamer for exportation to and consumption in Australia. Subsequently they gave us a performance of native solos and choruses, the latter being decidedly euphonious, and rendered remarkably effective by appropriate and graceful gesticulation. Most of the Fijian natives have been, at least nominally, evangelized, the Wesleyans and the Catholics having had missionaries at work amongst them for half a century. There is a dearth of good building stone in Fiji, and consequently Suva is mainly built of wood. An airy, open style of architecture prevails on every hand, the coolness and ventilation so desirable in a tropical climate being the objects chiefly aimed at by architect and builder. The population of Suva is of a somewhat miscellaneous character. There are about a thousand British inhabitants, but Fijians, Samoans, East Indians, half-castes, etc., are frequently encountered in the streets. At one time a large number of English settlers and a considerable amount of British capital were employed in developing the plantations of cotton, sugar, tea, coffee, and tobacco in Fiji, but during recent years the planters have been materially reduced in numbers, mainly in consequence of the difficulty of getting a regular and adequate supply of suitable labour. Another serious obstacle to the progress of the Colony is the fact that nearly all the land is held by the natives on the communal or tribal system, which results in protracted negotiations and ruinous delays before the intending settler can secure the land he desires. To this latter drawback Mr. S. M. Solomon, Q.C., the editor and proprietor of the *Fiji Times*, with whom I had a long and interesting conversation, attributed the comparatively unprogressive condition of the Colony during the past few years. However, it is not unlikely that the golden magnet will attract a considerable population to Fiji at no distant date. The precious metal has been known to exist in Fiji for some years, and at the time of our visit the most likely spots were being systematically prospected, with very satisfactory results. The parcels of gold that were sent down to Suva a few weeks ago certainly encourage the belief that our Crown Colony in the Pacific will soon take rank amongst the auriferous regions of the Empire.

Fiji is a Crown Colony of the severest type. The elective element is wholly and conspicuously absent from its administration. True, there is a small body called the Legislative Council, presided over by the Governor, but it has practically no power or authority; it simply registers the decrees of the Governor and of Downing Street. It passes legislative ordinances as a matter of form, these ordinances having been previously drawn up either by the Governor or the Colonial Office in London.

It consists of ten members, five of whom hold their seats as heads of the principal departments of the Civil Service, the other five being leading citizens nominated and appointed by the Governor as members of his Advisory Council. The latter frequently oppose the Governor's policy, but unavailingly, for, of course, the Governor and the official members can always command a majority when a division is challenged. The leading British settlers are anxious for some reform that would give them an effective voice in the government of the Colony; but until their numbers are appreciably increased, their desire for legislative emancipation is not likely to be attained. They are watching with great and sympathetic interest the progress of the Federation movement in Australia. Indeed, delegates from Fiji have taken part in the Federation conferences that have been held from time to time in Australia. The accomplishment of Australian Federation would undoubtedly involve a considerable change in the Constitution of Fiji. Its days as a rigid Crown Colony would be numbered, as the introduction of the elective element into its governing body would be an essential preliminary to its admission into the Australian Dominion. Governor Sir J. B. Thurston, who now reigns with Czar-like authority over Fiji, has been connected with the Colony in various capacities for close on thirty years. A native of Gloucestershire, he emigrated to New South Wales while a young man, and entered on a business career. While on a trading voyage amongst the South Sea Islands, his vessel was wrecked, and it was in a small boat containing the survivors of the catastrophe that he first entered the Colony where he is now the Queen's representative. He was appointed to a humble post in the British Consulate of Fiji, the group being at that time a native kingdom, under the rule of Thakombau. This dusky monarch tried the experiment of ruling on British lines, with a Parliament and responsible Ministry. Mr. Thurston became Chief Secretary and head of the Government in 1872, and he was largely instrumental in bringing about the annexation of the group to Great Britain two years later. Sir Arthur Gordon (now Lord Stanmore) was the first British Governor of Fiji, and Mr. Thurston became his right-hand man in the administration of the affairs of the new Colony. After holding the various offices of Colonial Secretary, Auditor-General, Consul-General, and Assistant High Commissioner, he succeeded to the Governorship in 1887. In addition to his duties as Governor of Fiji, he exercises a wide jurisdiction as Her Majesty's High Commissioner for the Western Pacific. Contrary to the rule and practice of the Colonial Office not to keep a Governor more than six years in the same Colony, Sir J. B. Thurston has had his term of office extended for a further period of four years, from which it would appear that Downing Street is desirous of availing itself as long as possible of his unique knowledge and experience of the Pacific Islands.

Suva rejoices in an excellent cricket-ground, and England's national game is now thoroughly acclimatized in Fiji. As this is a land of perpetual summer, the game is played practically the whole year round. But they are not such gluttons for cricket in Fiji as in the neighbouring group of Samoa, where matches of sixty or seventy a side, lasting a week, or even a fortnight, are not unfrequent. In Suva the principal patron and performer of the game is the Attorney-General, Mr. J. S. Udal, barrister of the Middle Temple. So proficient have they become with the bat and ball, natives and settlers alike, that a side was being organized for a tour of New Zealand and the Australian Colonies. Six members of the side, I was informed, would be Fijian chiefs. So it will be seen that a "Fijian Eleven" is one of the possibilities of the early future at Lord's and the Oval.

XI.

THE CENTENNIAL CITY.

Sydney, the starting-point of the British occupation of Australia, and the scene of several of the most important events recorded in colonial history, can now lay claim to comparative antiquity, for it has completed its first century, and has celebrated the occasion by the erection of the Centennial Hall, a monumental building ranking amongst the colossal edifices of the world. The western end of this capacious hall is occupied by the largest organ in existence, built specially by Messrs. Hill and Sons, of London, taken out to Sydney under the supervision of a member of that firm, and erected there at a total cost of 14,000*l*. To start this immense instrument on its career of glory and renown, Mr. W. T. Best, one of the most eminent of English organists, was brought out at considerable expense, and he delighted large audiences for some months with the wealth of harmony he evoked. Organ recitals continue to be given every Wednesday and Saturday in the Centennial Hall, and are extensively patronized. M. Auguste Wiegand, formerly of the Italian Church, Hatton Garden, London, now holds the office of City Organist of Sydney.

After an absence of seven years, I do not perceive any very striking changes in the external aspect of the parent Australian city. The most noteworthy, perhaps, is the invasion of American insurance companies, who are apparently competing with one another in the matter of erecting the tallest, the most expensive, and the most Chicago-like structures in the very heart of the business quarter of Sydney. These towering and eye-compelling edifices are, of course, mainly designed as costly advertisements. Each of them proclaims aloud: "Only a solid, substantial, prosperous, and enduring insurance company could afford to put up such a magnificent sky-scraper as this." But I heard on all sides that these enterprising Yankee insurance companies are very likely to burn their fingers in Sydney, and that there is not much probability of their diverting business to any appreciable extent from the old, steady-going, modestly-housed British and Colonial companies that have been established in Australia for many years. In Castlereagh Street, Lord Rosebery, who is a Sydney ground landlord as well as an Imperial statesman, has built a handsome establishment for the members of the Athenæum Club. Unlike its London namesake, the Sydney Athenæum is not composed in the main of bishops and "littery gents." A Colonial club, to fulfil the requirements of Mr. Micawber's balance-sheet that worked out satisfactorily, must aim at a comprehensive roll of membership. Hence, at the Sydney Athenæum Club one meets the foremost men in the political, journalistic, artistic, and commercial circles of the Centennial City. The late Premier, Sir George Dibbs, practically lives there during the currency of the parliamentary session, and many of the M.P.s find the Athenæum Club a very serviceable institution, for it is only a stone's throw from the unprepossessing, undignified, and uncomfortably cramped collection of wooden buildings, intended in the first instance for hospital purposes, where the collective wisdom of New South Wales has so long been accommodated. The contrast between the palatial freestone structures in which the Government Departments are housed in Sydney, and the meagre, unsightly rooms provided for both Houses of the Legislature, is certainly a tribute to the modesty, the self-denial, and the contempt for luxurious surroundings evinced by successive generations of chosen representatives of the people of New South Wales.

Although progressive and up-to-date in many respects, Sydney has not improved its system of street locomotion and suburban communication.

The same old hideously-ugly steam motors are still seen noisily and smokily drawing tramcars through the leading thoroughfares, in some places approaching within a few feet of the sidewalks, and constituting everywhere a ceaseless menace and a constant eyesore. The rivalry between Sydney and Melbourne is so keen and so pronounced that it is surprising to find the senior city allowing the younger one to monopolize the advantages and the benefits of noiseless, pleasant, and comfortable tramcars worked on the underground cable system. However, Sydney has made a beginning with this much-needed reform, and the work of reformation ought to be prosecuted vigorously until not a solitary steam-engine is seen running through the streets.

The advertising letter pillar-boxes are another abomination to the sensitive eye. These obtrusive outrages have been invented since I was last in Sydney. They are more than twice the height of the pillar-boxes standing in the streets of London, and the circumference is considerably enlarged as well, in order to provide as much advertising space as possible. Each advertiser, apparently, has the right of painting the space he has leased from the Postmaster-General any colour he pleases, and the inevitable consequence is a maddening medley of conflicting hues. You see somebody's soap extolled on a bright blue ground, while underneath the virtues of somebody else's pills are proclaimed on glaring red, and overhead a third party's boots are eulogized on a startling yellow surface. By similarly farming out the pillar-boxes of London and the principal provincial centres, the Imperial Postmaster-General could no doubt obtain an increase of revenue that would enable him to decree and to establish Imperial penny postage by one stroke of his pen and without the slightest danger of departmental loss, but I question very much whether the British public would consent to acquire even so great a boon at the cost of a new and ever-present advertising horror in their streets. All the world over the ruthless and aggressive advertiser is now despotically asserting himself, and there is a growing conviction that he ought to be summarily arrested and limited for the future to his legitimate sphere of operations. As most people are aware, Sydney Harbour is one of the most glorious pictures of panoramic loveliness that the earth can present, and yet some of its fairest spots are at this moment marred and disfigured by the irreverent and soulless advertiser, who regards the rocks and the headlands merely as good natural hoardings for the dissemination of information concerning his pills and his soap. Misconduct of this character, such offensive defilement of the beauties of nature, ought to be made a criminal offence.

During my visit Sydney was in a high state of indignation at the candid criticisms of Max O'Rell in his new book on the Colonies, copies of which had just arrived in Australia. The genial French humorist spent a couple of years in the Australian colonies, lecturing to lucrative and attentive audiences, and passing a very pleasant time. Nowhere was he received more cordially or listened to more respectfully than in Sydney, and it is therefore not surprising that the Sydneyites should feel hurt at the unkind things he has said about them in his book. For instance, he suggests that Sydney is an exceptionally immoral city, and this is indignantly repudiated by the Sydney press and public as a hasty generalization based on imperfect information and casual observation. There can be no doubt that disedifying and repulsive scenes obtrude themselves in the Sydney streets and parks both by day and night, but too much might easily be made of such unpleasant incidents, the fact being that from a moral standpoint Sydney is neither better nor worse than any other large and populous city of the British Empire. As regards the prevalence of drunkenness, to which the French critic-humorist also pointedly alludes, that is unquestionably a conspicuous feature of colonial life. The influence of the fifties and the sixties, when gold was plentiful and lucky diggers were legion, when conviviality was universal, and to refuse to drink with anybody, even with a total stranger, was regarded as a personal insult, survives to a considerable extent, and is largely responsible for the sociable free-and-easiness and the habitual readiness with which the Australians gather into drinking groups. "Shouting," the gold-diggers' slang expression for inviting all and sundry to drink, continues to be a colloquial phrase, and to typify a too general colonial custom in spite of all the efforts of temperance reformers to lessen and eradicate it. The evil is undoubtedly a very serious one, but local legislators do not seem disposed to treat it seriously. A Speaker of an Australian Parliament, who was remonstrated with for not putting the question from the chair in a loud enough voice, replied:—"It is no part of my duty to shout for honourable members." "I am sorry to hear you say so," came a voice from the back benches, and then the House laughed uproariously.

XII.

THE AUSTRALIAN G.O.M.

ALTHOUGH he is at present neither Prime Minister nor leader of the Opposition, the veteran octogenarian Australian statesman, Sir Henry Parkes, is still one of the most potent, and certainly the most picturesque figure in the political arena of Greater Britain. I found him decidedly dissatisfied with the sequel to the General Election in New South Wales, when, after having contributed powerfully to the overthrow of Protection and "enthused" the country from a score of platforms in favour of a return to the principles of Cobden and Bright, a Free-trade ministry was formed without his co-operation or concurrence. Sir Henry naturally resents what he regards as an unwarrantable piece of sharp practice, and the old parliamentary hand is credited with a determination to upset the ministerial apple-cart of the Hon. G. H. Reid, Q.C., at the first favourable opportunity. The alleged antipathy or lukewarmness of Mr. Reid towards the federation of the Australian colonies is being strongly emphasized by Sir Henry, and a coalition between himself and the leader of the straight Opposition, Sir George Dibbs, has been formed on a federal basis. It is true that Sir George is the leader of the defeated Protectionist host, and that Sir Henry was the man who mainly inflicted the defeat, still, that battle is over and gone, and as victor and vanquished are both out of office, they have agreed to bury the hatchet, join their forces, and form a coalition with Federation as its principal plank, watchword, and battle-cry.

Sir Henry Parkes having intimated that he would be pleased if I could spend an afternoon with him, I duly presented myself at his new residence, Kenilworth, Annandale, a pleasant Sydney suburb that offers two distinct advantages to a literary statesman—a pervading quietness by day and an easy distance from the halls of legislation. Kenilworth is one of a series of five detached villa residences, all built exactly alike, and each surmounted by a tapering spire—an architectural peculiarity suggestive of a little ecclesiastical group. As you ascend the staircase to the reception-room, you pass a splendid bust of Lord Tennyson, who for many years was the admiring friend and correspondent of Sir Henry. The late Poet Laureate entertained the Australian statesman-versifier more than once at his home in the Isle of

Wight, and their correspondence is both interesting and cordial. As Sir Henry enters and gives me a kindly greeting, I notice that while his figure is not so upright as in days of yore, and his voice is somewhat weaker and shriller, he has not appreciably altered during the seven years that have elapsed since I last set eyes upon him. The same capacious head, the same patriarchal profusion of impressive white hair, the same keen searching thought-reading glance, the same high-pitched voice, slow and deliberate utterance and wonderfully well-constructed sentences, considering that the speaker never had three months of consecutive schooling in his youth. Sir Henry is above all a self-educated man. He has graduated in the great school of life experience, the university of hard persistent up-hill work from foundry-hand in Birmingham and agricultural labourer in Australia to Prime Minister five times in succession, and the most influential personal force in Greater Britain. After conversing for a few moments on Australian federation, which in Sir Henry's opinion is advancing steadily towards the destined goal, the subject changed to Lord Rosebery, in whom the octogenarian is deeply interested. He was anxious to ascertain the prospects of Lord Rosebery's permanent leadership of the Liberal Party and the nature of the opposition to his Premiership within the Liberal ranks. I spoke optimistically as to the former, and added that the latter had been considerably exaggerated, whereupon the veteran looked pleased and went on to recall reminiscences of a very pleasant sojourn at The Durdans, Epsom, where he was the guest of Lord Rosebery, and one of a brilliant house party that embraced amongst others three literary Americans of high standing in the persons of James Russell Lowell, Henry James, the novelist, and G. W. Smalley, of the *New York Tribune*. Lord Rosebery drove Sir Henry all around Epsom in a dog-cart, and the veteran loves to linger over the recollections of these drives and the charming conversation of his host. Lord Carrington is another peer of whom Sir Henry entertains a high opinion. He expressed to me his great surprise that Lord Carrington had not received a better office in the Ministry than that of Lord Chamberlain. Sir Henry was Prime Minister during most of Lord Carrington's reign in New South Wales, and his opinion is that " Lord Carrington has far greater ability than the public or the leaders of the Liberal Party give him credit for." He added that he was much impressed by the tact, the discernment, and the statesmanly skill with which Lord Carrington had managed several difficult and delicate matters while Governor of New South Wales. As regards Robert Lowe (the late Viscount Sherbrooke), of whose election committee in Sydney in 1848 Sir Henry Parkes was secretary, I was somewhat astonished to hear the veteran expressing a not altogether flattering estimate. " Lowe was entirely wanting in two of the essential elements of real greatness. No man can be truly great who is without heart and sympathy. Lowe had neither. He had great readiness of repartee, a wonderful power of invective, an unsurpassed capacity for marshalling the facts of his case to the best possible advantage, and a vast mine of erudition to draw upon for similes, phrases, and historic parallels, but he was ever and always the professional advocate, and never once, even in his greatest and most memorable orations, did he touch the heart or the human emotions. Therein he was the exact antithesis of Gladstone. The secret of Gladstone's wonderful and long-continued power and popularity is to be found in his great heart and universal sympathies." While speaking thus Sir Henry was careful to point out that personally his relations with Lowe had always been of the friendliest kind. It was largely owing to the energy and canvassing ability of Mr. Parkes that Lowe was elected member for Sydney in 1848, and when Lowe had subsequently attained high rank in the Imperial Parliament he was always very gracious to his old Sydney friend when the latter visited England.

After some further conversation, Sir Henry asked Lady Parkes (who is an accomplished, well-informed, and vivacious conversationalist herself, and the possessor of a singularly musical voice) to produce those volumes of letters from celebrities of the century which are his greatest prize and delight. They are all handsomely bound, the name of the celebrity whose correspondence it contains being printed in large letters of gold on the cover of each. The Carlyle correspondence is the bulkiest of the series, for between the sage of Chelsea and the artisan Australian Premier there was a natural affinity which developed into a particular friendship, resulting in a most interesting correspondence covering a long period of years. The volume of Lord Tennyson's letters is next in size, and the one that is labelled "Gladstone" is also pretty thick, but of the latter it has to be observed that all the letters in it were not addressed to Sir Henry. He is an enthusiastic admirer of the English G.O.M., and has collected everything he possibly could that bears the signature "W. E. Gladstone." The first of Mr. Gladstone's letters in Sir Henry's collection is dated 1833, and the last was written during this present year of grace. There is also a letter from Mr. Gladstone's father, Sir John Gladstone. Sir Henry possesses one tremendously long letter from Daniel O'Connell, covering no less than eight large-sized sheets of paper, and in showing it to me he mentioned that he had heard O'Connell deliver three splendid speeches. John Bright, John Stuart Mill, Robert Browning, H. W. Longfellow, General Grant, and Richard Cobden also figure in Sir Henry's correspondence volumes, and he has besides a very large collection of autographed portraits of celebrities that must be of considerable monetary value; but although Sir Henry is notoriously a poor man, and has never succeeded in mastering the art of feathering one's own nest, notwithstanding that he has been at the head of five Ministries, and has been longer in power than any other public man throughout the Empire, yet he never means to part with any of these mementoes of his friendship and intercourse with the great men of the nineteenth century.

In a room downstairs, opening into a charming fernery arranged and constantly supervised by Lady Parkes, Sir Henry does his daily work, for though an octogenarian, he continues to ply his pen industriously and to produce sheets of neatly and closely-written manuscript with almost as much readiness and celerity as in the days of forty years ago when he was editing the Sydney *Empire*. This room is literally crammed with books, seemingly in utter confusion, but the octogenarian has a marvellous memory and can always put his finger on the book he wants. In a locked case standing in a corner are preserved a number of first editions and special presentation volumes,

Tennysonian and otherwise. On opening this case the first volume on which Sir Henry happens to alight is a first edition of Lord Byron's first volume of poems—"Hours of Idleness"—that was so savagely reviewed in the *Edinburgh*. Byron is one of his favourites, and he said he was sorry to hear it when I remarked that I did not think the author of "Childe Harold" was much read or appreciated in England nowadays. Then Sir Henry produced a first edition of his own little pioneer volume of verses—"Stolen Moments"—and with pardonable pride pointed out that it now ranked amongst valuable literary curiosities, a copy recently changing hands in Sydney at fifty times the original published price. Sir Henry has a complete collection of early editions of Leigh Hunt, whose writings he holds in the highest esteem. Sir Charles Gavan Duffy he admires as a "writer of luminous and clear-cut English." They are old Australian friends and fellow-statesmen, and moreover it was to Sir Gavan that Sir Henry was indebted for his first introduction to Carlyle.

Unquestionably an afternoon spent in the company of Sir Henry Parkes is a recollection to be treasured, for there is no other public man in the British Dominions who has triumphed so splendidly over the slings and arrows of outrageous fortune, and who has made good to so large an extent the accidental deficiencies of early education. By his own exertions Sir Henry has risen from the very lowest rung of the ladder to the very highest, he is entitled to take a place in the front rank of the Empire-builders of the century, he has materially moulded the destinies of the great branch of the Anglo-Saxon race dwelling beneath the Southern Cross, and has powerfully assisted in laying broad and deep the foundations of the future Dominion of Australia.

XIII.

PREMIERS, PAST AND PRESENT.

The late Prime Minister of New South Wales has apparently suffered not the slightest loss of good spirits, or the smallest diminution of his exuberant vitality, by the recent overthrow of Protection, and his Protectionist Ministry, at the polls. Calling upon him at his room in the ramshackle series of sheds that do duty for a Parliament House in Sydney, I found the legislative giant in a most affable, entertaining, and conversational mood. He is far from regarding the result of the late General Election as a knock-down blow to the principle of Protection. On the contrary, he believes that the State stimulation of local industries, with a view to providing constant employment for the people, is a policy that will be emphatically endorsed by the electors of New South Wales in the light of greater knowledge and wider experience than they now possess. He is not surprised that Sydney should have pronounced overwhelmingly in favour of a return to Free Trade, for, as the leading Australian seaport, its profit and its interests obviously lay in that direction. "I would be a Free Trader myself, if it was a matter of Sydney alone," he said to me, "but, when I consider the best interests of the country as a whole, my honest conviction is that Protection is the wisest and most salutary policy." As regards federation, Sir George still holds strongly to his scheme of unification between New South Wales and Victoria, and maintains that once these two most important of the Australian Colonies federate on the lines he has suggested, the inclusion of the others in the new Dominion would inevitably follow at no distant date. He was much pleased at the attention his unification scheme received in the English press, and he handed me, with evident satisfaction, a sheaf of extracts received the day before from a London Press-cutting Agency. Undoubtedly a great advance towards the goal of federation has been made since I was last in Sydney. The people then were lukewarm, indifferent, and apathetic; now they seem to realize the importance of this great national issue, and they manifest their awakened interest by crowding to the numerous meetings organized by the local Federation League for its promotion. It is beginning to be perceived that federation means a substantial reduction in the public burdens, a more economical administration of Governmental departments, and a sensible diminution of the extravagant absurdity of keeping up seven complete sets of Civil Services for less than four millions of people. At a time like the present, when the Australian Colonies are passing through a period of the severest depression, consequent on the unprecedented banking crisis of 1893, this argument from the standpoint of economic common sense in favour of federation comes home with a force and directness and conviction that were not possible in former years of abounding prosperity.

At the Mayor's luncheon in the Sydney Town Hall in October last, I was cordially cheered when I contrasted the economical administration of the federated Canadian provinces, through which I had just travelled, with the multiplied, overlapping, and costly Civil Services that prevailed amongst a much smaller but non-federated population in Australia. I agreed with Sir George Dibbs that Victoria and New South Wales ought to sink their minor differences, and set a good federal example to the rest of the Colonies. The jealousy that formerly openly and violently raged between New South Wales and Victoria, and more particularly between their respective capitals—Sydney and Melbourne—has undoubtedly cooled down considerably during recent years, and the efforts of Sir George Dibbs to completely extinguish the smouldering embers, and pave the way for a fraternal federal union, are deserving of success and entitled to the thanks of all well-wishers of Colonial progress. Sir George, it will be remembered, was the lion of the season in London a couple of years ago, and he speaks of his visit to the old land as one of the most agreeable recollections of his life. He met the Prince of Wales, was entertained at various country houses, participated in a number of Society functions in London, and was knighted by the Queen on the eve of his return to Australia. He has taken up very warmly the case of the *Costa Rica Packet,* a Sydney whaling barque, whose captain was summarily arrested by the Dutch authorities in the Moluccas, taken a thousand miles away from his ship, imprisoned in a loathsome, insanitary dungeon, discharged without trial, and left to find his way back to his ship as best he could. The unqualified vigour and emphasis of Sir George's telegrams to the Foreign Office in connection with this case made Lord Rosebery and Lord Kimberley shrug their shoulders and elevate their eyebrows considerably. They wanted to pursue the beaten paths of diplomacy, but, as Sir George Dibbs said to me, " What's diplomacy got to do with such a transparent outrage as this ? Make them pay for it. That's the only possible diplomacy in such a disgraceful and insolent business." Sir George is an old sailor himself, who has run the blockade more than once during the wars of the South American Republics, and this no doubt explains the ardour and honest indignation with which he goaded the Foreign Office into activity, and which were largely instrumental in compelling the Dutch Government to agree to arbitration in the matter of the captain, owners, and crew of the *Costa Rica Packet*. His early nautical associations are also responsible for the unconventional breeziness of Sir George's general conversation, and the easy familiarity with which he adapts himself to the society in which he happens to find himself for the time being. When he is not at the Athenæum Club or within the Parliamentary precincts, Sir George will be found at a picturesque retreat not many miles from Sydney, where he casts politics to the winds, and loves to recreate himself as a turner, carpenter, blacksmith, for he is fully qualified to practise any or all of these trades if ever he should fail to make a livelihood by commerce and politics. He learnt the art of turning in Darlinghurst Gaol, Sydney, where he was imprisoned for twelve months, on account of his refusal to pay what he believed to be an extortionate bill of costs. Afterwards, as Minister, he had the satisfaction of promoting his favourite warder to the position of governor of the selfsame prison. Frank, outspoken, pugnacious, obstinate, when he feels himself in the right, indifferent to criticism himself, and careless how his own criticisms affect other people, Sir George Dibbs is a strongly-marked, original character, who is pretty sure to find or make a way to the Treasury Bench again.

"The long and the short of it," one would be tempted to exclaim on seeing the late and the present Premier of New South Wales standing side by side. For Mr. Reid is almost as much below the average height as Sir George Dibbs is above it. He is a stout, rubicund little gentleman, with a Chamberlainian eye-glass and an attractive air of genial good-fellowship. His reputation in the past has been practically confined to his unswerving championship of Free Trade in season and out of season. His ability and pertinacity in this respect have charmed the Cobden Club, and led that body to shower all possible honours upon his head. He assumed the leadership of the Free Trade Opposition when the veteran Sir Henry Parkes somewhat petulantly threw it up, in the belief that he was indispensable, and would have to be sent for when the time came to form a Free Trade Ministry. That time arrived in due course, but the veteran was not sent for, and Mr. Reid successfully formed a new Ministry "off his own bat," a not inappropriate simile, seeing that Mr. Reid was once an ardent cricketer, still holds the office of President of the New South Wales Cricketing Association, and rarely misses an important match. Although one of the first acts of the Reid Government was to issue a circular letter to the other Australian Premiers, intimating that "this Government is prepared to take up, with genuine earnestness, the question of a united Australia," the intentions of Mr. Reid with respect to this important issue have given rise to no little speculation and some ominous shakings of the head. The fact is that Mr. Reid has yet to demonstrate his practical desire to promote the cause of federation, as hitherto his whole-souled devotion to Free Trade has left him but little time or inclination to help on and popularize other large questions of Colonial policy. His holding aloof from the federal propaganda is now his vulnerable point, and should he be prematurely displaced before he has a fair opportunity of displaying his administrative ability, it will be by a coalition Federal Ministry, headed by Sir Henry Parkes and Sir George Dibbs. He is the author of "Five Free Trade Essays," and "An Essay on New South Wales." In the latter work he argues very powerfully in favour of systematic emigration from the British Isles to the Australian Colonies. On it, he maintains, the progress of the Colonies practically depends. The Australian Colonies have immense area and capacity, and he declares it would be difficult to point to richer fields for the surplus labour and capital of the United Kingdom. "A community young yet conservative, pushing yet generous, free yet orderly," is his summing-up of the people over whom he now presides as Premier.

XIV.

RELIGIOUS SYDNEY.

FOR several weeks during my stay Sydney was the scene of a singular outburst of emotional religion, evoked by the impassioned utterances and fervid appeals of the Rev. John McNeil, the "Scottish Spurgeon" as he is sometimes called, who was minister of the Regent Square Presbyterian Church, London, a few years ago. Mr. McNeil is engaged on an evangelistic tour through the English-speaking world, and he is accompanied by a Mr. Burke, the possessor of a splendid singing voice, which is an invaluable aid to the musical portion of the services. Every day the Centenary Hall was thronged at noon, and the Exhibition Building in the evening, by thousands of men and women in a high state of spiritual exaltation. Most of them were evidently regular church-goers who had been stirred up out of the ordinary routine by the vivid, direct, and unconventional addresses of the "Scottish Spurgeon." The spirit of temporary revivalism, once started, becomes infectious, and is fanned by the reports in the newspapers, the huge placards on the walls, and the gossip of the trams and 'buses. In the booksellers' shops, prominently displayed in long rows, were to be seen cheap editions of the life of the "Scottish Spurgeon," showing how he rose from the humble position of a railway porter to the high office of a popular evangelist. Mr. McNeil's discourses in Sydney have been remarkable for their honest candour and blunt outspokenness. They have been largely concerned with the castigation of Colonial vices and failings. For instance :—" Poor demented Sydney. I can't sit down on a seat in the park, or a bench in my hotel, or rub shoulders with anyone in the street, without hearing betting, betting, betting—the Melbourne Cup, the Melbourne Cup—this horse and that. Man, be the thief you are—go and steal the money out of a fellow's pocket; be an honest thief if possible, but for the sake of all manliness be above betting. As the American put it, betting is about the measliest sort of thing that has escaped out of hell." Here's another illustration of Mr. McNeil's forcible way of putting things :—" Bullocks, when driven past a slaughter-house, will pause and sniff and tremble, because they smell the blood of their butchered kin. I tell you there is not a public-house, not an hotel bar, where you may not smell the blood of your butchered brother. Back in God's name. Back from the bloodstained threshold, and never cross it unless to bring some poor victim out in God's name." But Mr. McNeil surpassed himself in his scathing comments on the ballroom and ladies' evening dress :—" This mixing up of Christ with theatres, and balls, and gambling, and unclean speculation in business, is the ruin of all ye in Sydney. My brother, let me put it bluntly, you cannot stand to dance half through the night and on into the early morning with a more or less naked woman. I am speaking of the ordinary dress ball as it is—a thing of the flesh and uncleanness, the very conception and essence of it. Why, if you met your sister or your wife in that dress anywhere else you would hunt her home. You would send her home in a cab with the windows shut and the blinds down." These caustic observations aroused considerable controversy, and in some quarters occasioned no small offence. The *Sydney Morning Herald* published a leading article with the object of proving that dress, or the absence of dress, has really little to do with morality.

Concurrently with the revival of evangelistic fervour promoted by the breezy oratory of the "Scottish Spurgeon," Sydney witnessed a temporary recrudescence of the spiritualistic craze. The achievements of a local medium named Mrs. Mellon became the talk of the town, and at one of her *séances* no less distinguished a personage than Mrs. Annie Besant, the high-priestess of Theosophy, attended and assisted. Mrs. Besant was introduced by the medium to a materialized spirit as "one of the most famous women of the century." Mrs. Besant is said to have been profoundly impressed by her conversation with this materialized spirit, which tends to support Mr. Gladstone's suggestion in a recent number of the *Nineteenth Century* that she has not yet completed the cycle of her wanderings in search of a satisfactory soul-refuge. But at the *séance* immediately after the one that Mrs. Besant attended, the medium, Mrs. Mellon, was ludicrously bowled out. A Mr. Henry, himself an enthusiastic spiritualist, was inspired to suddenly rush forward and throw his arm around a "materialized spirit." The husband of the medium and three or four others assaulted him violently, and strove their utmost to pull him away, but he held his grip tenaciously until the candles were relit, when the "materialized spirit" within his grasp was found to be none other than the medium, Mrs. Mellon, herself. At the moment that the tableau was illuminated, she was endeavouring to conceal a black mask, false whiskers, and certain other useful aids to the manufacture of materialized spirits. The incident has been productive of considerable merriment to outsiders, while the small inner circle of believers in the possibility of manifestations from the other world have had their faith severely shaken. Curiously enough, the Mr. Henry who thus brought Mrs. Mellon's career as a medium to an unhappy and summary close is the author of a book called "Miracles in our Midst," which is in the main a credulous eulogy of all Mrs. Mellon's powers and feats as a medium, with photographs of the "spirits" that she materialized.

The Cardinal Archbishop of Sydney, whose health was very precarious while sojourning last year in Rome, London and Dublin, has become thoroughly convalescent under the influence of the genial climate and perennial sunshine of his cathedral city. In response to a kind invitation, I spent an afternoon at the imposing new palace he has built at Manly, a delightful spot near the northern head of Sydney Harbour. Many years ago the New South Wales Government granted several acres at Manly as a site for a Catholic college and Archbishop's residence, but neither Archbishop Polding nor Archbishop Vaughan (younger brother of Cardinal Vaughan of Westminster) took any steps to utilize the ground for the purposes specified. Cardinal Moran arrived just in time to save the land from resumption by the State with a view to its conversion into a popular reserve. He has expended close on one hundred thousand pounds on the erection of a magnificent college and a very attractive episcopal residence. The former overlooks the broad Pacific, and is the first building that greets the eye of incoming voyagers from

Canada and the United States. It is intended to be the great seminary or training-school of the Catholic Church in Australia. Hitherto comparatively few Australian Catholic natives have embraced the ecclesiastical life, and the ranks of the Catholic clergy in the Colonies have been mainly recruited from the Irish colleges in general, and All Hallows College, Dublin, in particular. The new college erected by Cardinal Moran at Manly is intended to demonstrate that the allegation that Australian natives have no vocation for the clerical calling is not founded upon fact. Pope Leo the Thirteenth is particularly interested in this new college, and has presented it with two gifts—an admirable portrait of himself in oils, for which he gave special sittings, and a valuable altar that has been erected in the college chapel. There is a very interesting museum of relics and curiosities of the early days of Sydney, mostly associated with Archpriest O'Flinn, who landed in Sydney at the beginning of the century, ministered secretly for a time to the Catholics of the place, but was afterwards arrested, imprisoned, and sent back to England because he could produce no official authorization to officiate in the Colony. His case evoked debates both in the Lords and Commons, and led to the appointment by the Imperial Government of a couple of Catholic chaplains for Sydney. A framed letter hanging on the college walls is another curious memento of those bygone days. It is an application from another pioneer priest for permission to go out to Australia, enclosing a testimonial from the local Protestant minister that he was a person of good character and repute. There is a picture of the modest edifice that was dignified with the name of St. Mary's Cathedral half a century ago, with a cottage that was called the " Bishop's Palace " adjoining, and in the foreground a group of aboriginals, one of the black women carrying a " piccaninny " on her back. Such a sight as that is no longer to be seen, for the blacks are almost annihilated by drink and disease, and the St. Mary's Cathedral of to-day, although not yet completed, ranks among the largest and finest ecclesiastical edifices of the world. Cardinal Moran is an enthusiastic antiquarian, and has written largely on the early British and Irish Churches. During the past three years he has been hard at work delving into the records, reports, correspondence, diaries, etc., bearing on the rise, growth, and development of Catholicism in the Colonies. The archives of the Vatican, the Propaganda at Rome, Westminster, Paris, Dublin, etc., have all been industriously searched, with the result that there will shortly be issued from the Cardinal's pen simultaneously in London, New York, and Sydney a " History of the Catholic Church in Australia," in two volumes, that will be full of hitherto unknown information and unpublished original documents. It is to be illustrated by 250 engravings, and, judging from the hasty glance I have had over the proof-sheets, it will be not only an important contribution to ecclesiastical history, but also the occasion of considerable controversy, for the Cardinal has penned some severe strictures on the Church of England, its conduct and its policy in the Colonies during the early years of the century.

XV.

THEATRICAL SYDNEY.

Mr. F. B. Chatterton, who preceded Sir Augustus Harris in the management of Drury Lane, is reported to have once sadly remarked from the stage of the national theatre that "Shakespeare spells ruin." An Australian manager gave expression to the same sentiment in a more roundabout, amusing, and unconventional style :—"You want Shakespeare, do you? Well, I gave a Shakepearian season lately, and went to some expense in mounting the plays, but that season was a dead failure. Legs and bright eyes with the limelight have eclipsed old Bill." Sir Henry Irving has abundantly proved that Mr. Chatterton was a little premature in making Shakespeare synonymous with bankruptcy, and Mr. George Rignold, lessee and manager of Her Majesty's Theatre, Sydney, has no less convincingly demonstrated that in Australia the ballet, burlesque, and the limelight have by no means succeeded in banishing "old Bill" from the boards. Mr. Rignold is a member of the well-known English theatrical family of that name, and may be said to have been born into the profession, his mother—a leading actress of half-a-century ago—having played with Macready and Phelps. Before settling in Australia, Mr. Rignold, who made his first appearance at the Theatre Royal, Birmingham, had gained the suffrages of the London playgoing public by his splendid performance of Henry the Fifth at Mr. Labouchere's theatre in Long Acre, and subsequently at Drury Lane. This is considered, and deservedly so, his finest Shakespearian character. "Henry the Fifth" has been repeatedly revived by Mr. Rignold in Australia, and invariably with pronounced success from every point of view. It was in that favourite character he commenced his management of Her Majesty's Theatre, Sydney, in November, 1887. This new, bright, and spacious Thespian temple has a large and deep stage that enables full justice to be done to the Shakespearian spectacular drama. In point of fact, the mounting of the national dramatist in Sydney, under the direction of Mr. Rignold, approaches very closely the high standard of splendour, completeness, and correctness of detail that are the characteristics of Mr. Irving's Shakespearian productions at the Lyceum. During my recent stay in Sydney, Mr. Rignold was playing Shakespeare's "Julius Cæsar" with an all-round ability, an accuracy of costume, and a wealth of scenic accessories that would have elicited the cordial approval of the most fastidious of London audiences. The character of Mark Antony Mr. Rignold has made his own in the Colonies, but he has also successfully assumed such diverse Shakespearian characters as Caliban, in "The Tempest," Bottom, in "A Midsummer Night's Dream," and Cardinal Wolsey, in "Henry the Eighth." In point of fact, more than half of Shakespeare's plays have been produced under Mr. Rignold's auspices in Australia—a fact that testifies strongly in favour of the culture of Colonial audiences.

The actor who, at the time of my sojourn in Sydney, was playing Brutus with sustained power and elocutionary effect to the Mark Antony of Mr. Rignold, is one of the veterans of the British stage, a member of Charles Kean's company during the famous Shakespearian revivals at the Princess's Theatre, London, and one of the few surviving actors who played before the Queen and the Prince Consort in the fifties. This interesting gentleman is Mr. James F. Cathcart. I had a very agreeable and instructive interview with him at his Sydney home—the Towers, Macquarie Street. Mr. Cathcart is stone deaf in the right ear, but this affliction is neither productive of personal inconvenience to himself, nor the source of any delays or drawbacks to the play in which he is appearing. His half century's connection with the stage has familiarized him so thoroughly with all the great dramas that

L

come under the general heading of the "legitimate" that he is almost independent of the five senses. An active, rubicund, medium-sized, white-haired, keen-eyed, affable gentleman, Mr. Cathcart converses on the recollections of the past with a clear, melodious voice, a distinctness of enunciation, and a precision of memory that leave nothing to be desired. Indeed, the colonial dramatic critics are constantly holding up Mr. Cathcart as a model for the imitation of the new generation of actors in the important matters of speaking so as to be heard all over the house, declaiming blank verse with propriety and correct emphasis, and acquiring a thorough mastery of the text. Mr. Cathcart is the son of a Dublin barrister, James Leander Cathcart, who took to the stage and became the leading actor on a circuit that embraced the town of Gosport (Hants). It was in this town that the Sydney actor of to-day first saw the light on Dec. 30th, 1828. His first appearance was as the boy, in "Pizarro," and on Dec. 4th, 1844, he played Lucius, in "Julius Cæsar," at the Theatre Royal, Glasgow, his father sustaining the character of Brutus. A framed day-bill of this performance is now in Mr. George Rignold's collection of theatrical curiosities. Before he had attained his majority young Cathcart had become known to Charles Kean, who engaged him in September, 1850, as a member of the London Princess's Theatre company.

Mr. Cathcart's connection with Charles Kean continued without interruption for the next eighteen years, and was only terminated by the death of that eminent actor. Half that period was spent at the London Princess's Theatre, where Mr. Cathcart played Nemours, in "Louis the Eleventh"; Laertes, in "Hamlet"; and Malcolm, in "Macbeth." At Drury Lane he played Iago to Kean's Othello, gaining much critical approval, and his impersonation of Stukely, in "The Gamester," was also generally admired. The latter nine years of Mr. Cathcart's connection with Charles Kean were spent principally in Australia and America. It was in October, 1863, that Kean and his company made their first Australian appearance at the Haymarket Theatre, Melbourne, under the management of Mr. George Coppin, now a member of the Upper House in Victoria. At the close of a lengthy and remarkably successful Melbourne season, they visited the Ballarat and Bendigo Goldfields, where their triumph was no less pronounced. In Sydney they played for a considerable period to crowded and enthusiastic houses. Finally Mr. and Mrs. Kean, Mr. Coppin, Mr. Cathcart, and other leading members of the company sailed away from Sydney to San Francisco in a trading barque. There were in those days no large and well-appointed steamers running to and fro as at present across the Pacific between Australia and America. The barque in which the Keans and Mr. Cathcart voyaged took no less than eighty-four days to cross the Pacific— a journey that is now regularly accomplished by steamers in less than three weeks. But the length of the voyage would not have mattered very much if the passengers were comfortable and had plenty to eat. Unfortunately this was not the case. The barque ran short of provisions and water, and for the last week of the voyage biscuits and potatoes were the sole sustenance available. Mr. Cathcart says that for eight successive days he had to utilize the same water for washing purposes. Mrs. Kean suffered severely during this time of privation, and Mr. Kean offered the captain a considerable amount of money if he would make straight for the nearest port, Honolulu, but that surly navigator refused to adopt such a reasonable suggestion, and kept on his erratic course to San Francisco, for the steering, both Mr. Cathcart and Mr. Coppin agree, was of a very peculiar and eccentric description. However, they entered the Golden Gate at last, famished, weary, unwashed, but still alive. They were compensated for all their trials and tribulations on the Pacific by cordial receptions and crowded houses in all the chief American cities.

Mrs. Keeley, the "Grand Old Woman" of the English stage, is a very old friend and correspondent of Mr. Cathcart. They played together in the early fifties, and a recent photograph of the venerable lady, with a kindly greeting duly autographed, is displayed by Mr. Cathcart with pride and pleasure. With Lady Theodore Martin, the Helen Faucit of bygone years, he was also professionally associated; and at Manchester he acted with a novice who is now at the head of the profession—Sir Henry Irving, to wit. Mr. Cathcart many years after saw Mr. Irving play Mathias, in "The Bells," during the Bateman management at the Lyceum, and he declares that it was "one of the finest and most impressive performances he ever witnessed."

XVI.

A CITY OF FALLEN GREATNESS.

The metropolis of Victoria is named after the Queen's first Prime Minister, Lord Melbourne, who derived his title from the little Derbyshire village of that name. A story is told of a pompous and wealthy Melburnian from the Southern Hemisphere who visited the Derbyshire hamlet, and astonished the villagers with his tales of the riches and magnificence of the populous new Melbourne that had sprung up on the other side of the world. "Ah, well," remarked a venerable old inhabitant, when the Australian visitor had finished his glowing recital, "our Melbourne was in existence centuries before yours, and it will be in existence centuries after yours has passed away. Such mushroom cities as yours don't last." The first thought that occurred to me while strolling round the Victorian metropolis, after an absence of seven years, was that the old Derbyshire villager's prophecy had already commenced to operate. The collapse observable on every side is both painful and phenomenal. Stagnation, depression, despair are the three words that sum up the sadly altered situation in Melbourne. The loss of population is something enormous. An exodus of sixty thousand souls during the past eighteen months is officially acknowledged, but this estimate falls considerably short of the reality. Judging from the immense number of closed shops and untenanted houses that I witnessed during a systematic tour of the suburbs, some figure between 100,000 and 150,000 would more correctly represent the astounding decrease in the population of Melbourne—that is to say, practically a third of the inhabitants of the metropolitan area has disappeared. Suburban streets that I remembered as crowded and busy hives of industry are now simply long rows of silent, unoccupied, and dilapidated shops. In the city proper most of the shops are still open, but offices in the huge piles of buildings that were reared aloft in the "boom" days are now a veritable drug in the market. Hundreds of them are vacant, many are let at merely nominal rents, and not a few can actually be had rent free. Tenants everywhere are masters of the situation. Rent is a mere courtesy to owners, who are glad to accept whatever tenants care to offer. In most of the outlying suburbs rent is a disestablished institution, owners being only too happy to have respectable people occupying houses in the capacity of caretakers until the arrival of better times, for they know the fate that has overtaken a host of the unoccupied houses of Melbourne—wreck, mutilation, and the carrying away of everything portable.

The whole history of the circumstances that have contributed to this gloomy transformation of the "Marvellous Melbourne" which Mr. George Augustus Sala delineated in terms of superlative admiration a few years ago would take a long time to write. But, to put it briefly, it may be said that, while Melbourne is by no means deficient in the natural conditions of progress and legitimate development, its prosperity in the past, striking, colossal, and stable as it seemed to be, was, in reality, largely built on an unreal and artificial foundation. In the fifties and sixties it reaped most of the advantages of the immense influx of gold-diggers *en route* to Ballarat, Bendigo, and other up-country goldfields. Melbourne was their port of arrival, their holiday-making arena when they had more gold than they could conveniently carry, and the place in which many of them settled down after a time. In the seventies Protection became the fiscal policy of the country, with the result that factories and workshops of all sorts were concentrated in Melbourne, and the provincial districts depleted to such an alarming extent that, practically, half the population of the Colony at one time were aggregated within the metropolitan area. This unnatural state of things could not possibly last. In the eighties a ring of speculators started a land boom in Melbourne that attained dimensions wholly undreamt of by its originators. The craze for buying and re-selling city and suburban lands developed into downright mania. All classes of citizens, from the highest to the lowest, plunged into the whirlpool of speculation, and the great majority of them were, in the end, engulfed so completely that their heads are still under water, and years must elapse before, commercially speaking, they will be able to breathe freely again. When the boom was at its height, land and house property in Melbourne and its vicinity were artificially forced up to values vastly in excess of what they would bring if situated in the most eligible quarters of London. It was quite an ordinary occurrence to buy a property to-day and to re-sell it at an advance of 10,000*l.* or 20,000*l.* to-morrow. All the paddocks, farms, gardens, and open spaces within a radius of twenty miles around Melbourne were snapped up by syndicates, mapped out into sub-divisional allotments, and disposed of by auction, in the presence of excited crowds of spectators brought to the spot in gorgeous vehicles, and regaled on arrival with champagne luncheons. And it was not individuals alone that completely lost their heads—the banks, building societies, and finance companies, not only speculated wildly and largely on their own account, but by reason of the accommodating facilities they afforded to their directors, friends, and influential private speculators, were potent factors in creating and prolonging this extraordinary boom.

A time came when this towering edifice of rapidly-generated and seemingly universal wealth and prosperity appeared to reach the clouds, and then it collapsed with startling and dramatic suddenness like a house of cards, or bills, as it really was. Banks, unable under the circumstances to withstand continuous and panic-stricken runs upon their available monetary resources, had to close their doors and suspend payment; building societies, hopelessly involved in the ruins of the boom, had similarly to confess themselves unable to meet their obligations, whilst the number of mushroom "finance companies," "mercantile corporations," "land banks," etc., to which the boom gave birth, and which vanished from the scene in an aroma of fraud, scandal, and exposure, would take some time and trouble to calculate. For, when the bubble burst and the truth was revealed, it was found that much of the financing during the boom period was of the shadiest possible description. A few scapegoats were seized, tried, and sentenced to various terms of imprisonment, but, as the investigations proceeded, it was discovered that they were no worse than hundreds of others, and when it became evident that public men, leading merchants, etc., had done things during the rush, and fever, and excitement of the land boom that could not be defended or justified before a judge and jury, the highest influence and the greatest possible pressure were brought to bear upon the authorities, with the result that the extinguisher was clapped upon further prosecutions, and "Let bygones be bygones" became the general and accepted watchword. The line that separates a smart, speculative, enterprising business man from a criminal is proverbially a thin and narrow one. There are many sobered, ruined, and repentant erstwhile "land boomers" in Melbourne to-day who shiver as they realize how easy it was to overstep that line, and are thankful that things are no worse with them.

Melbourne is now suffering a recovery from the feverish excitement and fictitious prosperity of the "land boom" era. The absolutely unsaleable land in all directions that a few years ago changed hands repeatedly at an advance of thousands of pounds each time; the immense array of untenanted houses in the suburbs; the huge piles of unoccupied offices in the city proper; the great decrease in the population; the general, omnipresent air of depression—all represent the morning headache after the night's dissipation. And like the headache in the individual, Melbourne's present affliction is only of a temporary character, although from the pessimistic, despairing tone in which some Melburnians talk, an uninformed listener might easily be led to a different conclusion. The fact is that the present unprecedented depreciation in land and property in and about Melbourne is as unnatural and as abnormal in its way as was the unreal and artificial inflation of the "boom" years. It is a case of the higher the ascent the deeper the fall. Melbourne is the metropolis of one of the richest Colonies in the Queen's dominions—a Colony lavishly endowed with auriferous, agricultural, pastoral, commercial, and manufacturing resources still largely undeveloped—and the British investing public need have no fear as to its future, and as to satisfactory returns in good time for the capital they have placed there.

XVII.

THREE "BOSS BOOMERS."

You cannot find a single man in Melbourne who has profited by the "land boom." There are any number who say they could and would have made a fortune if they had realized and retired at the right time, but their heads were too intoxicated by seeming success and by the all-pervading atmosphere of excitement in which they lived, and moved, and had their being, to recognize the psychological moment for retreating with safety and a competency for life. They could no more keep away from the daily land-gambling whirlpool than the moths from the flame of the candle or the birds from the glare of the lighthouse. The temptation to make a few thousands more by another deal was always irresistibly egging them on, until the day came when the huge bubble burst and they found themselves in many instances worse than penniless, with monetary obligations that they could not possibly meet, calls on shares in land and finance companies that they could not satisfy, and heaps of unproductive houses and unsaleable

estates thrown on their hands. Hardly one of the
"bosses" of the boom, the public men and mercantile magnates who started the mania and supplied it with motive power until the community in general caught the infection, has survived or emerged in a solvent condition. Some are in gaol serving sentences for fraudulent practices in connection with the boom; others are fugitives lying low in various quarters of the world; but most of them have either gone, or are going through, the whitewashing process of the bankruptcy courts.

Beyond a doubt, Sir Matthew Henry Davies, Knight Commander of the Order of St. Michael and St. George, who has received his certificate of discharge from the judge of the Court of Insolvency in Melbourne, was the "Prince of the landboomers." There are some who hold that he, aided and abetted by the British investing public greedy for ten or twenty per cent. on their money, was the real and original author of the boom. That is perhaps a little too far-fetched a theory, but it is undeniable that the immense amounts of money that were thrown at the head of Sir Matthew by British investors, and which he largely invested in the acquisition of suburban lands and properties, played a prominent part in paving the way for the boom. Sir Matthew must have seemed an ideally safe man to the average British investor. Speaker of the Parliament of Victoria, member for the most wealthy and aristocratic suburb of Melbourne, President of the Y.M.C.A., a shining light in the religious world, a regular contributor of a thousand pound cheque on Hospital Sunday, the distributor of ten thousand pounds amongst the Melbourne charities, a generous patron of the Imperial Institute in South Kensington, the chairman of a Royal Commission on banking, and by repute the soundest and most successful financier in the southern hemisphere—if these were not satisfactory guarantees of safety, security, and good interest, where was the British investor to look for them? And yet at the present moment unpopular is a mild word with which to characterize the relations of Sir Matthew towards the British investor. Most of the banks, land corporations, and finance companies, into which hundreds of thousands of British capital were thrown on the strength of Sir Matthew's name and reputation and his official connection with them, collapsed with the bursting of the boom, and the unfortunate British investor was left lamenting. Sir Matthew himself was subjected to a series of criminal prosecutions, brought back to Melbourne in custody from Ceylon while *en route* to England, and eventually acquitted after having been on the rack for a couple of years. Now, after his meteoric career as the "Prince of land-boomers," during which he occupied a gorgeous mansion, fraternized with Viceroys and entertained on a princely scale of magnificence, he lives unknown and unnoticed in a five-roomed house somewhere in the suburbs. He has returned to the practice of his old profession as a solicitor, which he is heartily sorry he ever abandoned for the more dazzling but dangerous *rôle* of the colossal land-boomer. There are few, if any, contemporary lives better calculated to point a moral and adorn a tale than that of Sir Matthew Henry Davies.

The downfall of the Hon. James Munro, a gentleman who was once Premier of Victoria, Agent-General for the Colony in London, President of the Melbourne Total Abstinence Society, and the "Sir Wilfrid Lawson of Australia," is hardly less striking and significant. After holding for some twenty years a high place in Melbourne as a successful politician, a founder of banks, and a pioneer of building societies, he has dropped completely out of public notice, and is swallowed in the obscurity of a little suburban rent-collecting agency. He, too, was very favourably regarded by the British investor, especially to the north of the Tweed. The Federal Bank of Australia, which was chiefly established by the energy and influence of Mr. Munro, which collapsed shortly after the bursting of the boom, and which is now in liquidation, received a considerable amount of Scottish support and capital. When Mr. Munro visited London five years ago he was at the zenith of his fame as a financial expert and banking authority, and he had no difficulty in carrying through several schemes of considerable magnitude, so great was the confidence reposed in him in the City. At the end of 1890 he became Premier of Victoria, giving his Government the title of the "National Liberal Ministry." Early in 1892 he retired from the Premiership with the object of establishing himself in London as Agent-General, but he was only a few months in Westminster when he was requested to return to Melbourne and explain his relations to certain collapsed financial institutions with which he had been prominently identified. He did so, and was soon overwhelmed by a succession of failures of banks and companies in which he was heavily interested. The Real Estate Bank, which he founded at the beginning of the land-boom, involved himself and many of his confiding friends in ruin and disaster. He has received his certificate of discharge in bankruptcy, and at the age of sixty-three is manfully starting life afresh to repair his broken fortunes.

Every tragedy has a comical incident of some sort, and amid the ruin and desolation produced by the land-boom in Melbourne, the reduction of many a family from affluence to penury, the sweeping away of many an industrious man's life's savings at one fell swoop—amid all the havoc and misery entailed by falling banks and crashing

M

corporations, the serio-comic figure of the Hon. Thomas Bent makes fitful appearances on the tragic stage from time to time and illuminates the sombre scene with a ray of grim humour. His conversion of himself into a limited liability company—" The Thomas Bent Land Company " — was certainly calculated to give what the dramatic critics call "comic relief" to a very serious drama. Whether he plagiarized the idea from Mr. W. S. Gilbert, or whether the latter's famous Duke of Plazo-Toro was suggested by and modelled on a living Australian original, is a question that has never yet been definitely and satisfactorily determined. Mr. Bent's transactions during the boom period were of a multitudinous and comprehensive character. He seemed to be an indispensable constituent of every syndicate. Originally an illiterate, ungrammatical market gardener at Brighton, a marine suburb of Melbourne, he succeeded in ousting from the representation of that borough the late George Higinbotham (afterwards Chief Justice), one of the greatest parliamentary orators and political leaders that the Colonies have produced. The defeat of a statesman of Mr. Higinbotham's character and standing under such circumstances constituted the greatest surprise on record in the political history of the Antipodes. In the Victorian Parliament Mr. Bent energetically pushed his way, first to the Treasury bench and eventually into the Speaker's chair. Every member confessed that Mr. Bent was the least qualified for the latter high office, but Mr. Bent was determined that he would wear the full-bottomed wig and gown, and he achieved his object by persistent whipping and skilfully playing off diverse sections of the House against each other. A legislative body presided over by a Speaker eminently suggestive of the comic-opera stage went perilously near becoming an extravagant burlesque on representative institutions. But Mr. Speaker Bent was rejected at the late general election, certain peculiar transactions of his, in connection with the land-boom that came to light shortly before polling-day, being understood to have turned the scale against him. Like Sir Matthew Davies, Mr. Munro and other "boss boomers," Mr. Bent has thus been exiled from the political arena for the present, but his characteristic enterprise and audacity will doubtless discover an opening again before long. In the meantime his Gilbertian venture is amongst the breakers. Proceedings for the winding-up of the "Thomas Bent Land Company" were in progress while I was in Melbourne. A witness who was asked for what amount he would sell his shares, replied, with scornful surprise : "Sell! You can have them for nothing."

XVIII.

THE PARLIAMENT OF VICTORIA.

The *façade* of the Victorian Houses of Parliament has been completed since I was last in Melbourne, and a long and spacious flight of steps leading to a handsome pillared porch now decorates the eastern end of Bourke Street, the principal commercial thoroughfare of the metropolis. This porch gives admission to the Queen's Hall, in the centre of which is one of the late Sir Edgar Boehm's statues of Her Majesty. This hall serves as a conversational lobby for members and their friends. Portraits of Speakers in their full robes of office look down from the glistening white walls. Unlike the new Palace of Westminster, the Victorian Houses of Parliament are surrounded by spacious and secluded gardens. The Victorian Speaker is thus enabled to entertain members and their friends in a manner that is not possible to Mr. Speaker Gully, who may, and does, give dinner-parties at Westminster, but who is precluded from giving garden-parties there. The Speakership of Sir Matthew Davies, now an impecunious and burst-up land-boomer, was a downright carnival in this respect. According to tradition, one of his garden-parties, given at the height of the boom, in honour of the visiting viceroys of the Southern Hemisphere, cost the pretty little figure of five thousand pounds. Subsequent Speakers have wisely refrained from giving such ruinously expensive garden-parties, and lawn-tennis now represents the highest form of dissipation to which the Parliamentary gardens are devoted. On the southern side of the Parliamentary buildings is a smaller garden, more open to the public gaze. In its centre is an elaborately-sculptured stone fountain which has a curious history. It is the work of a prisoner while serving a long sentence for bushranging, or robbery under arms, to employ the title of Rolf Boldrewood's famous Australian novel. This prisoner developed quite a talent for sculpture during his incarceration, and on his release he established himself in business in Melbourne as a monumental mason. He succeeded from the first, kept to honest courses ever afterwards, and died an honourable and respected citizen, having completely lived down the recollection of his early criminal career. A still more striking instance in this connection is that of a Speaker in an Australian Parliament, who had a skeleton in his closet in the shape of a conviction and term of imprisonment some thirty years previously. One afternoon an hon. member arose with a venerable-looking newspaper cutting in his hand, and proceeded to inform the horrified House that he proposed to read a report of the trial and sentence of the Speaker. There was, of course, an immediate uproar, and various attempts were made to silence the audacious ghoul. But the Speaker himself interposed with remarkable self-possession and dignity, quietly remarking that "the hon. member is perfectly in order; it is purely a question of taste." And so the curtain rose on the strongly dramatic situation of a Speaker —the first commoner of an important Colony— seated with wig and gown in his chair of state and having to listen to the record of his own trial and consignment to prison in the distant past. It must have been a terrible trial to the nerves of the Speaker in question, but he successfully emerged from the ordeal, and lost nothing in public estimation by reason of the gratuitous and uncalled-for exposure of his early indiscretion. Indeed, it was the industrious raker-up of a long-buried and forgotten scandal who had most reason to regret the incident. In the Colonies, when a man has lived an honest and honourable life for a period of twenty or thirty years, there is a general feeling of disgust and repugnance when some intrusive busybody proceeds to point out that he was not always what he is now. Gratuitous mischief-makers of that sort, together with too-enterprising police and detectives, who revel in the raking up of "former convictions," and in whispering to employers the names of ex-convicts who are striving to lead an honest life, are really more criminal themselves than the persecuted people whom they seek to injure and expose.

The present Victorian Parliament is presided over by that veteran statesman, Sir Graham Berry, who represented the Colony in London from 1887 to the end of 1891. Sir Graham has aged very much since he left London, financial troubles, no doubt, being chiefly responsible for the change. He was largely interested in one of the defunct institutions—the Mercantile Bank of Australia— and was a member of its London board. Sir Graham discards the orthodox wig and gown at ordinary meetings of the Legislative Assembly, and only appears in full official dress at important functions when the representative of Her Majesty is in attendance. Another ex-Agent-General in London has returned to public life in the present Victorian Parliament, after a long exile, in the person of Mr. Murray Smith, who represented Victoria in London from 1882 until 1887. At the close of his ambassadorial term he was entertained at a largely-attended banquet in the Freemasons' Tavern, under the presidency of the Duke of Cambridge. Mr. Murray Smith, who is one of the few Oxford M.A.'s in colonial public life, is an uncompromising and unswerving leader of the Free Trade cause, and, as Victoria is a pronouncedly Protectionist colony, he is as the voice of one crying in the wilderness. But his voice is a remarkably eloquent one, and it is safe to say that Mr. Murray Smith is a gentleman who would command attention and hold an interested audience in the House of Commons itself. His unvarying courtesy to opponents, his uniformly gentlemanly manner and bearing, and the classical correctness of his English, are sure to have a distinctly beneficial and educative effect on a House so largely composed of young, ardent, and impulsive members as is the present Victorian Legislative Assembly. Mr. Alfred Deakin, the foremost Australian native statesman, is another Victorian Parliamentarian who would undoubtedly shine in the House of Commons. His oratorical powers are of a very high order: indeed, his skill and brilliancy as a debater won compliments from so keen and competent a judge as the Marquis of Salisbury, who heard Mr. Deakin more than once during the sittings of the Colonial Conference of 1887 in London. Mr. Deakin is an advanced Radical, an ardent Federationist, and a Protectionist champion. He declined the knighthood that was offered him at the close of the first London Colonial Conference. Latterly, he has been devoting more attention to his growing practice at the Victorian Bar than to the pursuit of politics; nevertheless, he is one of the most potent personalities in the public life of Greater Britain, and, as he is still under forty, a long, brilliant, and fruitful career may be confidently predicted for him, especially if he should make up his mind to transfer his great natural gifts and stores of acquired information to the larger and more conspicuous stage of Westminster.

The Victorian Parliament has one blind member in the person of Mr. McKenzie, who, notwithstanding the deprivation of sight, takes a prominent part in its proceedings. He is a very effective speaker, and the possessor of a retentive memory that enables him to quote facts and figures with singular accuracy. It was he who moved the resolution of want of confidence in the Ministry of Sir James Patterson, and while I was in Melbourne he tried to upset the Government formed by Sir James's successor, but failed to repeat his former success, although he did withdraw several members from their Ministerial allegiance. The new Victorian Premier, Mr. Turner, is an amiable-looking lawyer and a ready speaker, but whether he has sufficient practical knowledge of finance to rescue the Colony from its present troubles and clear away the formidable deficit of close on five millions, remains to be proved. His ablest and most popular colleague is the Postmaster-General, the Hon. John Gavan Duffy, eldest son of Sir Charles Gavan Duffy, whose promised autobiography, "My Life in Two Hemispheres," is being looked forward to with much interest. Mr. J. G. Duffy is one of the wittiest and brightest speakers in colonial public life. A young member who has made a very promising *début* is Mr. W. H. Irvine, a nephew of one of the most celebrated Irish rebels of the century, John Mitchel, who was convicted and transported to Tasmania in 1848 for heading the revolutionary movement of that year, and who, after four years of exile, succeeded in escaping to America. Mr. Irvine was educated at Trinity College, Dublin, joined the Irish Bar, and is now a prosperous junior in the Melbourne Courts. His maiden speech in the Parliament of Victoria won encomiums from all sides. The Labour Party constitute an important group sitting on the Ministerial benches below the gangway. They act together as a rule, but, like their brethren in the House of Commons and elsewhere, they seem unwilling or unable to formally range themselves under a recognized leader. The principles of democratic equality apparently prohibit anything in the nature of official leadership. Nevertheless, merit and ability will come to the front, and Messrs. Trenwith and Hancock, by force of character and debating skill, are practically the directors of the Victorian Labour Party. Mr. Hancock, who sits for the working-class suburb of Footscray, is a Londoner by birth, a compositor by trade, and an orator by virtue of constant attendance at Cogers' Hall, off Fleet Street. He was a member of the composing staff of the *Standard* for five years, and thus had frequent opportunities of learning the art of public speaking amongst " ye Ancient and Honourable Society of Cogers," on the opposite side of Fleet Street. He is a very advanced Radical; indeed, he is now quite accustomed to being pelted by his opponents with such epithets as Communist, Nihilist, incendiary, &c. Strange that such an ultra-Democratic M.P. should have been developed in such an intensely Conservative quarter as Shoe Lane!

XIX.

LITERARY MELBOURNE.

UNLIKE London, Melbourne has no society that affixes tablets and inscriptions to houses in which literary men of distinction have lived. And yet not a few eminent writers have sojourned in Melbourne since the discovery of gold in 1851. Richard Hengist Horne, the friend and correspondent of the Brownings, a poet himself as well as a prolific prose writer, arrived in Melbourne in 1852, and almost immediately received the command of the escort that conveyed the gold from Ballarat to the metropolis. He subsequently blossomed into a gold-laced commissioner in charge of the McIvor Goldfield, and on his return to England recorded his colonial experiences in an interesting work, entitled "Australian Facts and Prospects." He was followed in 1857 by Charles Whitehead, a poet, novelist, and dramatist, who, in London, had enjoyed the friendship and esteem of Dickens, Thackeray, Leigh Hunt, Douglas Jerrold, Monckton Milnes, &c. It was to him that Chapman and

Hall first suggested the writing of "Pickwick," but he declined the offer, and indicated his young friend, Dickens, as the man best qualified for the work. Unfortunately, Whitehead became a victim to habits of intemperance in London, and although during his five years' residence in Melbourne he did some good work in the local papers and magazines, he eventually succumbed to his fatal weakness. After a prolonged drinking bout he was picked up insensible in the streets one morning, and conveyed to the Melbourne Hospital, where he died absolutely unknown and unbefriended. He was buried as a pauper, and his last resting-place in the Melbourne Cemetery has never been definitely ascertained. But a striking literary monument to his memory has been erected by Mr. Mackenzie Bell, in the shape of a study of his character and works, under the title of "A Forgotten Genius." Henry Kingsley, younger brother of the famous Canon, was a contemporary of Horne and Whitehead, and an occasional resident in Melbourne during his five years' vagabondizing in Australia. But, although he led a somewhat erratic existence in Australia, Henry Kingsley kept his eyes and ears open wherever he wandered, and the accuracy of description and fidelity of portraiture in his Australian novels have never been surpassed. His "Geoffrey Hamlyn" is regarded by Rolf Boldrewood and other good judges as the "finest Australian novel ever written." Rolf Boldrewood himself spent his boyhood in Melbourne, where his father, Captain Sylvester John Browne, of the East India Company's service, was a pioneer settler. Marcus Clarke, whose realistic romance of the transportation era, "His Natural Life," combines with Henry Kingsley's "Geoffrey Hamlyn" and Rolf Boldrewood's "Robbery under Arms," to form the classical trinity of colonial works of fiction, spent the whole of his literary life in Melbourne, occupying for several years the post of Sub-Librarian in the Melbourne Public Library.

But it is amongst the ladies of Melbourne that most literary activity prevails at present. The Melbourne male authors have mostly transferred themselves to London, and so have several of the successful lady writers, but there are enough young ladies of literary capacity and laudable ambition still resident in Melbourne to form an agreeable and prosperous club of their own, under the title of the "Austral Salon." According to the rules and regulations, the object of this organization is the "intellectual advancement of women," and "membership is limited to women actively engaged in literature, science, and the fine arts." A certain number of males are allowed within the charmed, or, rather, charming, circle, provided they are "in sympathy with, and willing by personal effort and influence to promote the objects of the Salon." Regular meetings are held on the first Thursday of the month, at which lectures are delivered, or original plays produced, or discussions held on questions of literary or artistic interest. But every Monday afternoon there are informal meetings, the leading members in turn playing the part of hostess and entertaining members' friends and distinguished visitors. Rudyard Kipling and Robert Louis Stevenson have been present at these Monday afternoon functions, and I was similarly privileged. The club-room is a handsome hall upstairs, in a new arcade connecting Collins and Elizabeth Streets. A picture of the Countess of Hopetoun, the President of the Salon, is conspicuous at the platform end of the apartment, and a library, largely composed of Australian authors and authoresses, fills some space on the right. Opposite the library is a refreshment bar, at which, however, not even so strict a body as the London County Council could take offence, as only the mildest non-alcoholic beverages are dispensed there. Seated in a capacious arm-chair, in the centre of the hall, sits the hostess of the afternoon, while in radiating lines around her are to be seen some sixty or seventy of the fair and intellectual daughters of Australia sipping tea, and either conversing on topics of feminine interest or listening to the music and recitations. Of course, the whole of this interesting company was not composed of authoresses, but many, if not most, of those present had either seen themselves in print, or looked forward with hope and pleasure to doing so in the immediate future. No less than seven young ladies with whom I conversed had books completed, and were negotiating with London houses for their production during the coming year. The success of "Tasma" and Mrs. Mannington Caffyn—both erstwhile residents of Melbourne, has evidently encouraged and developed no small amount of literary activity amongst aspiring ladies at the Antipodes. One Australian lady novelist, who has made her mark in London and become a favourite at Mudie's and Smith's, has refrained from emigrating to the banks of the Thames, contrary to the now established custom in such cases. "Ada Cambridge" lives at Williamstown, a marine suburb of Melbourne, where her husband, the Rev. G. F. Cross, is incumbent of the local Anglican Church.

Melbourne is a city of pleasant, well-lighted, and commodious arcades, but the most striking and attractive of them all is the colossal Book Arcade, which Mr. E. W. Cole has built up from very small beginnings. It is a unique institution. There is nothing to equal it in the world. Fancy a three-storied edifice running right through from street to street, with miles of shelves crowded with books old and new in every possible department of knowledge, not to mention some five thousand cedar drawers labelled with authors' names or special subjects. It is one of the great sights of the Southern Hemisphere. At all hours of the day, and up to ten o'clock at night, it is crowded. It is practically an informal public library, as Mr. Cole provides books, lighting, and seating accommodation to thousands, not to speak of the orchestral concerts which are given in the Arcade during the afternoons as an additional attraction. Mr. Cole estimates that he has ordinarily more than a million of books in stock, and, judging from the immensity of the establishment, and the skill with which every available inch of space is utilized, the estimate is by no means an exaggerated one. The founder of this huge literary emporium was born at Woodchurch, Kent, sixty-three years ago, and was attracted to Australia by the gold discoveries when he was in his twenty-second year. He spent ten years in the diverse capacities of gold-digger, wood-splitter, builder, cordial manufacturer, carpenter, cane-worker, and photographer. Then he came to Melbourne, and commenced business with a barrow-load of second-hand books in the Eastern Market. He gradually established a reputation as a purveyor of cheap and popular literature, moved from shop to shop as his business extended, and eventually found himself in a position to erect the capacious and attractive Book Arcade, running from Bourke to Collins Streets, with which his name and enterprise will long be associated. But Mr. Cole is an author as well as a leviathan bookseller. In his early years he projected a work on "The Origin of Religions," and collected a large amount of material bearing on this interesting, but also formidable, investigation. He has not been able to complete this work in its entirety, but portions of it have been published separately under the titles of "A Sketch of the Religions and Sects of All Nations," "A Sketch of the Sacred Scriptures of All Nations," "The Real Place in History of Jesus and Paul," "The Difficulties of the Deluge," and "An Essay in Defence of Mental Freedom." As a compiler he has also been industrious, and his collections of the thousand best poems, songs, humorous stories, &c., have had a large sale in England and America, as well as in the Colonies. As an example of the self-educated, energetic, dauntless, and versatile type of colonist, Mr. Cole is a very interesting and suggestive personality. Possibly he may still further widen the scope of his enterprise before long, and establish a Book Arcade in Piccadilly, just to show old-fashioned Londoners how the selling of books can be popularized, made attractive to the million, and brought right up to date. Spiers and Pond came from Melbourne to revolutionize the eating business in London. Similarly, Mr. Cole may one day wake up and astonish Albemarle Street and Paternoster Row.

XX.

RELIGIOUS MELBOURNE.

SHORTLY before my arrival Melbourne lost one of her most interesting and picturesque figures in the person of the Very Rev. Hussey Burgh Macartney, who had been the Anglican Dean of the City for the long period of forty-three years, and who continued to preach and perform his regular functions almost up to the day of his death, when he was well advanced into his ninety-sixth year. With him passed away the one surviving link that connected our times with the days when a Parliament was wont to meet in Dublin. His father, Sir John Macartney, Bart., sat in the last Irish House of Commons, and the future Dean of Melbourne was born in Dublin in April, 1799, the year before the Union was carried. For a quarter of a century he served as a minister of the Protestant Church in Ireland, and then he accompanied the first Anglican Bishop of Melbourne, Dr. Perry, to Australia. He witnessed the growth of Melbourne from a mere villgae of a few hundred inhabitants into a metropolis of half a million; he saw pastoral solitudes swiftly and almost magically transformed into huge, noisy, bustling, gold-mining camps, and he laboured hard and made long and toilsome journeys to minister to the requirements of his people during the early years of colonization in Victoria. His horror of Ritualism and aversion to undraped statues were characteristics that made him the object of satire and reproach from time to time. His rooted antipathy to High Church principles and practices was heartily shared by the first Bishop of Melbourne, Dr. Perry, during whose reign of twenty-seven years no sympathizer with the Oxford Movement could get an appointment in the Diocese of Melbourne. The *régime* of his successor, Dr. Moorhouse, now Bishop of Manchester, was an era of toleration to all schools of thought within the Church of England. The ten years during which Bishop Moorhouse governed the Diocese of Melbourne represent the highest point of influence and importance that the Anglican Church in the Colonies has so far attained. His exceptional gifts and powers as a preacher and platform speaker; his whole-hearted identification with the social reforms and elevating movements of his time; his keen practical intelligence and sterling common sense, together with the conscientious care and unwearying zeal that he displayed in regularly visiting even the remotest and least accessible districts of his vast diocese—all combined to give him a position in the estimation of the colonial public of all denominations that no other Anglican prelate has been able to attain. His successor in the bishopric at Melbourne, Dr. F. F. Goe, late Rector of St. George's, Bloomsbury, the church with the singular statue-crowned steeple in front of the British Museum, is an easy-going, common-place sort of prelate, with no aspirations or qualifications to become the potent and influential force in the community that Bishop Moorhouse was. His only excursion from the ordinary routine of episcopal duty was to engage in a controversial skirmish with the Catholic Archbishop of Melbourne, Dr. Carr, on "The Origin of the Church of England." Dr. Carr was Bishop of Galway when Mr. Parnell made his famous descent upon that city, and carried the election of Captain O'Shea, in spite of the strong opposition of Mr. T. M. Healy, Mr. J. G. Biggar, and others who foresaw the calamitous consequences of Mr. Parnell's connection with the O'Sheas. It is seven years since Dr. Carr was translated from Galway to Melbourne, and during that time he has practically completed the erection of St. Patrick's Cathedral, the finest ecclesiastical edifice in the Southern Hemisphere. Occupying a commanding site on the summit of the eastern hill of Melbourne, it has been forty years in building, and its total cost does not fall far short of a quarter of a million. Archbishop Carr is popular amongst all denominations. He is a genial and accomplished speaker, a scholar of considerable and varied erudition, and a scientist of no mean attainments.

As there is no State Church in the Colonies, it follows, as a necessary consequence, that such words as " Dissenters " or " Nonconformists " can have no place in a colonial dictionary. The religious bodies that are so designated in England stand on a footing of perfect equality in Greater Britain with the Anglican denomination. Or perhaps it would be more correct to say that they have raised themselves considerably above the level of the Anglicans, for in many places the Independents, the Wesleyans, and the Baptists have the superior places of worship, and pay their clergy much better stipends than fall to the lot of the average Anglican parson. Anglicans get so accustomed to being spiritually spoon-fed by the State, that when they emigrate to the Colonies they feel like fish out of water, become demoralized and parsimonious, and rarely acquire the art of doing as others do, putting their hands into their own pockets regularly every week for the support of their own religion. The Rev. Dr. Bevan, the pastor of the Collins Street Independent Church, the cathedral of colonial Congregationalism, draws a much higher stipend than the Anglican Bishop of Melbourne. Indeed, at the present time of writing one Australian Anglican diocese is threatened with extinction by reason of want of funds to pay the Bishop's salary. Dr. Green, Bishop of Grafton and Armidale, summoned his synod to meet and discuss the advisability of continuing the independent existence of the bishopric. The religious indifference, the lethargy, and the lack of self-reliance, induced by the establishment of a State Church, are points and arguments that the Liberation Society could drive home with telling effect from a systematic study of the Church of England in the Colonies. The aforesaid Rev. Dr. Bevan, who ministered for some years in Highbury, London, has attained a position of considerable influence in Melbourne, and is regarded as a sort of antipodean Spurgeon. The newest of the imposing ecclesiastical edifices erected in Melbourne bears the comprehensive but not particularly suggestive title of the "Australian Church." It was founded by the Rev. Charles Strong, an ordained minister of the Established Church of Scotland, and the friend and pupil of Principal Caird, on whose recommendation he was appointed to the pastorate of the Scots Church, the handsomest and the wealthiest Presbyterian Church in Melbourne. He had not been long in the Scots Church pulpit when the heresy-hunters were on his track, and an article of his on "The Atonement," in the *Victorian Review*, furnished material for charges of heterodoxy that were tried and debated in the Church courts for years, and eventually ended in the severance of Mr. Strong's connection with the Presbyterian Church of Victoria. A testimonial of £3000, to which people of all denominations subscribed, was presented to him on the eve of his return to Scotland, as a mark of sympathy and public esteem. He did not, however, remain long in Scotland. Coming back to Melbourne, he organized his friends and adherents into a new and original body, under the style and title of the "Australian Church," of which he is still the minister. However opinions may differ with respect to Mr. Strong's religious views, as a practical philanthropist and an earnest worker amongst the Melbourne poor and afflicted, his is a widely known and honoured name.

Many strange things happened during the land-boom in Melbourne, and not the least curious or remarkable was the revolution by which the Y.M.C.A. and the Secularists changed places. The Y.M.C.A. came to the conclusion that their modest hall and rooms in Russell Street were not adequate to their requirements, and so they purchased the Hall of Science in Bourke Street, at which atheists and blasphemers were wont to hold forth on Sundays. Having knocked down the Hall of Science and some contiguous buildings, the Y.M.C.A. erected on the vacant site a palatial edifice at a cost of £55,000. But, alas! the mortgagees were compelled to foreclose, and the new splendid building of the Y.M.C.A. passed into the possession of the Salvation Army for the small sum of £19,500. In the meantime, the evicted Secularists had found a home in the old rooms of the Y.M.C.A., so that the latter luckless body was in the unfortunate position of not being able either to retain their new and extensive premises or to return to their old and modest apartments. They are now temporarily housed in a flat in Collins Street. The extent and intensity of the "boom" mania in Melbourne are strikingly evidenced by the fact that even the Y.M.C.A. lost their heads, entered into engagements that they could not fulfil, became bankrupt and homeless, and have now to start their corporate life afresh, and build up a new organization out of the ruins of the old.

XXI.

THEATRICAL MELBOURNE.

QUEEN STREET is now only a second or third-rate Melbourne thoroughfare, but in the pre-goldfield era it was the principal artery of the Victorian metropolis. In the forties it was the scene of several sanguinary riots caused by collisions between the admirers and the detesters of King William the Third, and which led to the passing of the Peace Preservation Act, a measure that absolutely prohibits any secret society marching through the streets of Melbourne. The only reminder of its vanished dignity and primeval importance that Queen Street now possesses is a large, dilapidated, cavernous edifice, with the Royal arms, faded and crumbling, but still conspicuous on its front elevation. This building, now used as a coach factory, was the Queen's Theatre, the most famous and prosperous of the early Thespian temples of Melbourne. It was built by the Hon. John Thomas Smith, the Sir Richard Whittington of the Southern Hemisphere, for he was Mayor of Melbourne no less than seven times. When he came to London in 1858 and presented her Majesty with an address of congratulation from her loyal subjects in Melbourne on the occasion of the marriage of the Princess Royal to the late Emperor Frederick of Germany, he confidently expected to be told to "rise, Sir John Thomas," but the expectation was not realized, and he returned as he came—a plain Mr. He arrived in Melbourne originally as an accredited Church of England teacher; but he soon discovered a surer and quicker way to fame and fortune by providing the infant metropolis with its first regularly organized and permanent playhouse. Not only he himself, but his principal tragedian as well, Mr. Morton King, an erstwhile favourite in the English provinces, secured seats in the Victorian Parliament, and held them for many years. A unique performance of "Hamlet," in which all the male characters were played by members of Parliament, Mr. King himself taking the rôle of the melancholy Dane, realized £1000 for the Melbourne charities. The discovery of the goldfields in 1851 rapidly transformed Melbourne from a small town into a big city, and Queen Street was left stranded from the theatrical point of view. Bourke Street became the great commercial thoroughfare, and in or near it all the Melbourne theatres have ever since been concentrated. The one with the most interesting historical memories is the Theatre Royal, of which Barry Sullivan was for several years the lessee and manager, and on whose stage G. V. Brooke, Edwin Booth, Joseph Jefferson, Charles Mathews, Walter Montgomery, Sir William Don, Charles Kean, Madame Ristori, Dion Boucicault, Genevieve Ward, and other luminous stars from the Northern Hemisphere have shone from time to time during the past forty years. The newest and most attractive of the Melbourne theatres is the Princess's, close to the eastern end of Bourke Street, and almost directly opposite the Houses of Parliament. It is identified with the principal Australian triumphs of the London Gaiety company, headed by Nellie Farren and the late Fred Leslie. The former is understood to have pronounced it the "finest theatre in the world." Its principal lessee and manager, Mr. J. C. Williamson, graduated on the American stage and came to Australia some twenty years ago. Associated with his wife (Miss Maggie Moore) in a Dutch-American melodrama called "Struck Oil," he achieved an instantaneous and enduring success in the Colonies. His career as a manager, in partnership with Mr. Arthur Garner and Mr. George Musgrove, has been one long series of successes, not the least of them being the production of the whole of the Gilbert and Sullivan operas, in a style and with a cast but little, if at all, inferior to the original presentation at the Savoy. Like London, Melbourne has now a superabundance of theatres, and yet new places of entertainment are in process of erection, apparently in the sanguine belief that the clouds of depression will soon lift; that Melbourne will regain her lost hundred thousand of population, and that the amusement-loving world will become as active and as money-spending as in the light-hearted years that preceded the bursting of the "boom."

At his pleasant suburban retreat, Pine Grove, Richmond, I had the pleasure of meeting the veteran and versatile pioneer of dramatic enterprise in Australia, the Hon. George S. Coppin, M.P. Born into the theatrical profession at Steyning, Sussex, seventy-five years ago, Mr. Coppin played through the English provinces while still a youth, and was for some time a member of a company headed by James Sheridan Knowles. In his twenty-fourth year he emigrated to Australia, arriving in Sydney at the beginning of March, 1843, and appearing shortly afterwards at the Victoria Theatre in that city. Mrs. Coppin, a talented, powerful, and accomplished actress, played the title-rôle in Richard Lalor Sheil's well-known tragedy "Evadne," and Mr. Coppin, in one of those humorous afterpieces in which he subsequently became renowned, achieved an instantaneous and abiding popularity. As M. Puzzi, in "The Young King;" Peckover, in "The Contested Election;" Tony Lumpkin, in "She Stoops to Conquer;" Bob Acres, in "The Rivals;" Chrysos, in "Pygmalion and Galatea;" Daniel White, in "Milky White;" and Crack the Cobbler, in "The Turnpike Gate," Mr. Coppin had no rival on the Colonial stage, and his Paul Pry was pronounced by good judges to be fully equal to any contemporary representation of the character on the London boards. At the close of his Sydney season Mr. Coppin proceeded to Tasmania, where he organized a dramatic company and crossed over the Straits to Melbourne to open the aforesaid Queen's Theatre. His first Melbourne season was a pronounced success, and encouraged him to visit Adelaide, the metropolis of the neighbouring colony of South Australia, where he built a theatre in five weeks. He was getting on famously there when the news arrived of the discovery of large quantities of gold in Victoria. Adelaide was swiftly depopulated by the intelligence of so much wealth so easily got, and Mr. Coppin was left alone and temporarily ruined. But he soon pulled himself together again, and followed the crowd. As he himself tersely and humorously observes, "I returned to Melbourne, walked to the diggings without a sixpence in my pocket, and walked back again within a fortnight with blistered hands, a backache, and no gold." After this deplorable failure as a digger, Mr. Coppin resumed his old profession and played a successful star engagement in Melbourne. Thence he proceeded to Geelong, a place of considerable importance by virtue of its being the nearest seaport to the Ballarat goldfield. Entering into management as lessee of the Geelong Theatre Royal (now the local headquarters of the Salvation Army), Mr. Coppin was enabled to retire after two years with a large fortune. Revisiting old England, he appeared at the Haymarket Theatre, London, in a round of his favourite low-comedy characters, and won the cordial approbation of the critics. He subsequently went on a starring tour through the provinces, playing with great success in Birmingham, Manchester, Edinburgh, Dublin, &c. At Manchester he met one of the most distinguished and versatile actors of the Victorian era in the person of Gustavus Vaughan Brooke, whom he engaged for a tour of the colonies. While in England he also superintended the construction of an iron theatre, which was taken out to Melbourne in pieces, and put together in a few weeks. It flourished for several years under the official designation of the Olympic, and the colloquial title of the "Iron Pot." G. V. Brooke became the most popular and successful actor that ever visited Australia, and his Shakspearian performances continue to this day to be the chief standard of critical comparison in the colonies. Mr. Coppin and Mr. Brooke entered into partnership in Melbourne and made a large amount of money by their theatrical enterprises, but the establishment of a Melbourne Cremorne and the ambitious determination to outrival the glories of its London prototype ended in failure, collapse, and ruin. The engagement of Mr. and Mrs. Charles Kean set Mr. Coppin on his legs again. He accompanied the Keans all over Australia and America, and when he returned to Melbourne he was in a position to become the principal proprietor of the Theatre Royal, with which he has ever since been intimately identified. Notwithstanding that he has now attained the age of seventy-five, Mr. Coppin continues the active performance of his duties as managing director of the Theatre Royal, and is in daily attendance at that popular establishment.

Mr. Coppin is not only an actor-manager, but a prominent public man and enterprising citizen to boot. As far back as 1858 he was elected a member of the Victorian Upper House, and from 1874 to 1889 he sat in the popular chamber as member for East Melbourne. He is now back again in the Upper House as the representative of the metropolitan province. With the passing of two very salutary measures through the Victorian Parliament—the Transfer of Real Property Statute and the Act for the creation of Post Office Savings Banks—his name is honourably identified. As founder of the Old Colonists' Association, which provides homes for deserving pioneers who have fallen on evil days, and of the Dramatic and Musical Association, which similarly comes to the relief of necessitous players and vocalists, Mr. Coppin is also entitled to praiseworthy recognition. Nearly all the philanthropic agencies and charitable institutions of Melbourne number him as a benefactor, and, altogether, the career of Mr. George Coppin may be commended to the thoughtful consideration of the short-sighted people who contend that nothing in the nature of good citizenship or exemplary character can ever come out of the theatre.

XXII.

SOME MELBOURNE NOTABILITIES.

In the persons of Sir Anthony Colling Brownless and Sir Archibald Michie, Melbourne possesses a couple of interesting octogenarian knights. The former, who is a native of Kent, was a student at St. Bartholomew's Hospital, London, sixty years ago, and, as he was admitted to the distinction of M.R.C.S. of London as far back as 1841, it follows that he must have very few seniors in the British medical profession. Sir Anthony practised in London for several years, but the great tide of emigration consequent on the discovery of the goldfields carried him out to Australia in 1852. Melbourne was not able to accommodate a tithe of this immense influx of population, and thus it came about that an extensive suburb, entirely composed of tents, sprang up like magic on the southern side of the city. It was in this extemporized camping-ground, very appropriately christened Canvastown, that Dr. Brownless commenced to exercise his medical and surgical skill at the Antipodes. He was kept very busy while Canvastown lasted, and when the great rush of immigrants from every land under the sun had subsided, he transferred himself to Melbourne proper, where he not only established a large and lucrative practice, but also filled the office of Physician to the Hospital and Benevolent Asylum. For more than forty years his name has been inseparably associated with the rise and progress of the University of Melbourne, an institution to which he has devoted ceaseless toil and self-sacrifice. He founded its medical school, and when the Right Hon. H. C. E. Childers transferred himself in 1857 from Colonial to British public life, Dr. Brownless succeeded him as Vice-Chancellor of the University. He was promoted to the Chancellorship in 1887, and notwithstanding his advanced age, he still continues the active discharge of the duties of that highest of academic offices. He received his knighthood in recognition of his services to University education in Australia, and the honorary degree of LL.D. was conferred upon him by the University of St. Andrew's for the like reason.

The second octogenarian knight, Sir Archibald Michie, first saw the light in Maida Vale in 1813. His father, a London merchant, sent him to Westminster School, and as soon as he attained his majority he entered at the Middle Temple. He was called there in May, 1838, so that he must be one of the fathers of that particular Inn of Court. The year after his call found him a voyager to the

distant Antipodes. He tried his fortune first in
Sydney, where he had as a brother advocate at the
local Bar a young, white-haired, semi-blind, erudite,
silver-tongued, ex-Oxford tutor, who was destined
in after years to make his mark in the House of
Commons. Robert Lowe (Viscount Sherbrooke)
and Mr. Michie became close friends, and when
Lowe started his brilliant, but at times vitriolic,
Sydney weekly, the *Atlas*, Michie was one of his
earliest and most constant contributors. He is
now the sole survivor of the exceptionally gifted
literary staff that Robert Lowe organized in Sydney
for the production of the *Atlas*. With the
opening-up of the Victorian goldfields, and the
erection of a new self-governing colony in that
quarter, Mr. Michie moved from Sydney to Melbourne. He immediately became not only a
leading barrister, but also a prominent public man
in the new Colony of Victoria. He sat in its
popular Legislative Chamber for many years, and
was a law officer of the Crown in three Ministries.
As a Parliamentary wit he was held in high repute,
and his encounters with Sir Charles Gavan Duffy,
the Opposition humorist, were always gleefully
followed by a crowded House. Sir Gavan once
dubbed him "Mickey Free," a well-known
character in one of Charles Lever's novels, and the
name stuck. From 1873 to 1879 Sir Archibald
Michie officially represented Victoria in London,

receiving a knighthood at the close of his term of office. Sir Archibald was a very popular lecturer in his prime, and as Melbourne correspondent of *The Times* for many years he produced a series of sparkling letters on Australian affairs.

Although Mr. R. S. Smythe has his permanent home in a charming eastern suburb of Melbourne, he is quite as likely to be met with in London, New York, Cape Town, Simla, or Hong Kong, for he is known to fame as the "much-travelled manager." However, I was lucky enough to catch him "at home" during my visit to Melbourne. His handsome house—Highgate-on-the-Hill—commands a complete panoramic view of Melbourne, while in the opposite direction a series of verdant, undulating valleys spread out to the distant blue-clad mountain ranges. On the walls of the drawing-room are displayed a series of autographed portraits of the celebrities whom Mr. Smythe has from time to time piloted through Greater Britain—Archibald Forbes, G. A. Sala, H. M. Stanley, R. A. Proctor, Charles Santley, Max O'Rell, and Mrs. Besant amongst the number. In the library Mr. Smythe discloses several literary curiosities. In early life he was a corrector of the Press in London, and in that capacity went through the proofs of a number of famous books. He retains and exhibits the original proof-sheets of the now well-known "Curiosities of London," by John Timbs, the first issue of which he professionally saw through the press. He was also associated with the production of some of Carlyle's works, and he still has in his possession a number of marginal notes in the handwriting of the Chelsea philosopher. Mr. Smythe came to Melbourne forty years ago, and for seven years was an active and versatile pressman in that city. He edited the first pictorial journal published in Melbourne—the *Illustrated Post*—and did a considerable amount of musical and dramatic criticism. From pronouncing judgment on public performers he passed on to taking them under his managerial wing. He boldly struck out a number of new and unbeaten paths, and now rejoices in the knowledge and the recollection that he was the first manager to take a company to Japan, to Simla, and beyond the Orange River in South Africa. But for the past twenty years he has been chiefly connected with lecturing celebrities, whom he has accompanied all over the Colonies. To Mr. Smythe the educated public of Greater Britain are deeply indebted for the privilege of hearing some of the ablest speakers and seeing the most interesting personalities of our time.

Melbourne is the home of the "Clement Scott of the Colonies," to borrow the complimentary phrase by which Dr. J. E. Neild is not unfrequently designated. For forty years he has combined the practice of medicine and dramatic criticism with distinguished success. He is the life and soul of the Melbourne Shakspeare Society, and a veritable walking cyclopædia on all matters appertaining to the stage. He was the intimate friend of R. H. Horne during the latter's Australian residence, and he sheltered for a long time under his hospitable roof that brilliant but wayward genius, Charles Whitehead, whose melancholy fate in Melbourne I have referred to in a previous chapter. Dr. Neild, who is a Yorkshireman by birth, and a graduate of London University, is a witty and sparkling conversationalist, and one of the most genial and cultured of the worthies of Melbourne.

Mr. James Smith, the *doyen* of Australian journalism, also has his home in Melbourne, where his brilliant and versatile pen has been continually active for more than forty years. The early years of his journalistic life were spent in London, where he contributed to *Punch*, aud became the friend and pupil of Douglas Jerrold. Soon after his arrival in Australia, in 1854, he was largely instrumental in founding *Melbourne Punch*, which he edited for some time. Mr. Smith has been Parliamentary librarian of Victoria, has lectured on a variety of subjects, has produced half a dozen books, and he may be truly styled the Antipodean Sala, from the amazing number of entertaining and well-informed articles and sketches he has contributed to the Melbourne press.

No one is better known or liked in Melbourne than Mr. E. G. Fitzgibbon, the Chairman of the Metropolitan Board of Works. The dark clouds of corruption, disgrace, and disgust behind which the London administrative body of that style and title sank below the horizon have not deterred the Melbourne folk from starting an institution with the same ill-omened name. So far no word of reproach or suggestion of misdoing has been levelled against it. The Melbourne ratepayers have every confidence in its chairman, and implicitly rely on "Fitz" to keep it in the straight and honest path. "Fitz" is a native of Cork, and claims the Irish title of the "White Knight of Kerry," but his claim is contested by several Fitzgibbons in other parts of the world. There was a prolonged controversy on the subject during my stay in Melbourne, and the amount of valuable space the papers lavished on pedigrees of various branches of the Fitzgibbon family and consequential genealogical lore, was an index to the importance that the local head of the clan had acquired in Melbourne. Mr. Fitzgibbon was an officer of the Education Committee of the Privy Council when he resolved to emigrate to Victoria in 1852. He tried his luck as a gold-digger for a year, but as fortune obstinately refused to smile on his efforts in that direction, he retraced his steps to Melbourne, where he soon found an opening for his abilities as assistant to the Town

Clerk. In 1856 he succeeded to the Town Clerkship. He publishes weird poetry from time to time, and cherishes the conviction that he has annihilated Henry George by throwing a weighty and thunderous pamphlet at the head of the San Francisco sage.

XXIII.

SOME MELBOURNE INSTITUTIONS.

IN no city throughout the British Empire is labour so thoroughly and systematically organized as in the metropolis of Victoria, a fact to which the large and imposing block of buildings, collectively known as the Trades Hall, bears ample and conspicuous testimony. Within this capacious artisans' club, erected on a splendid site freely gifted by the State and fronting one of the leading thoroughfares of the city, every trade has its appointed room and hour of meeting. Friday evening is reserved for the Trades Hall Council, the supreme controlling body, composed of duly-elected representatives of the hundred affiliated trades, and empowered to legislate on all matters affecting the general interests of labour. This council or informal labour parliament naturally attracts to itself the cream of the debating power and intellectual ability of the trade-unionists, and from its benches the ranks of the labour party in the Parliament of Victoria are mainly recruited. The debates of the

Melbourne Trades Hall Council really attain a high standard of excellence, penetration, and well-informed speaking, and forcibly suggest the reflection that if the artisans and labourers of England were similarly highly organized, a potent and influential labour party would soon make its presence felt on the floor of the House of Commons. The Melbourne Trades Hall dates from the fifties, and was the outcome of the movement successfully initiated by the building trades forty years ago to secure the eight hours' day. In point of fact, the extension of the eight hours' day and the progress of the Trades Hall have gone hand in hand. They stand to a considerable extent in the relation of cause and effect. As soon as a trade won the eight hours' day, with the active assistance and co-operation of the other organized trades, it naturally fell into line and affiliated itself to the Hall in order to strengthen its position, consolidate its forces, and conserve the victory it had won. The third Monday of April is the great annual festival of the Trades Hall. It is Eight Hours Day, and all the associated trades, with banners waving and bands blaring, march through the streets of Melbourne in long and picturesque procession, considerable expense being incurred in some instances, not only to provide artistic banners, but also to arrange appropriate and effective tableaux. As a street spectacle, the Eight Hours procession in Melbourne is vastly superior to the weather-beaten, incongruous, and ill-timed pageant that is provided for the delectation of Londoners on the ninth of November. A pathetic feature of the Melbourne procession is the small body of grizzled pioneers of the eight hours' day who lead the van, and whose number diminishes year by year. Soon there will not be a solitary survivor, and at the head of the procession the only reminder of the pioneers will be their original modest little banner, not much larger than a good-sized handkerchief, bearing the inscription in plain capital letters: " Eight Hours Labour. Eight Hours Recreation. Eight Hours Rest."

Melbourne has a large and commodious central Temperance Hall, that was for many years the radiating centre of an enormous amount of evangelistic energy and activity directed towards the destruction of the traffic in intoxicating drink. But the events and exposures that supervened on the bursting of the land-boom have done much to discredit the temperance cause in Melbourne. It was shown conclusively in the courts that the men who were figuring constantly before the public eye as temperance leaders and social reformers, and denouncing the vice of drinking in all the moods and tenses, were themselves steeped to the eyes and ears in the vice of gambling, founders of wildcat banks, and reckless speculators on a colossal scale in city and suburban lands. Hundreds and thousands of families who placed implicit confidence in these colonial imitators of Jabez Spencer Balfour, and who invested their little all in so-called banks and financial institutions, managed by the conspicuous chiefs of the religious, temperance, and philanthropic worlds, are now totally ruined, and bitterly deplore the day on which they first came under the influence of such fanatical temperance reformers and financial leaders to destruction. It will thus be easily understood that the Temperance Hall is not a particularly popular institution in Melbourne at present, but the influence it has exercised in the past is strongly stamped on the liquor legislation of Victoria. The colony possesses what Sir Wilfrid Lawson has so long and so unavailingly clamoured for—a local option law—and also a rigorous Sunday Closing Act. The former has been put into operation in several districts by the vote of the ratepayers, but the results have by no means come up to anticipations. A certain number of public-houses have been closed, and substantial compensation has been awarded by a judicial tribunal to both owners and licensees, but the expected diminution of drinking and drunkenness consequent on these proceedings has not ensued. The patrons of the compulsory-closed hotels simply transferred their custom to the nearest open " pub." The unanimous testimony of the police is that the local option law has had practically no effect as an instrument of social and temperance reform. A much greater measure of success has been achieved in the matter of Sunday closing. No doubt a very appreciable amount of Sunday trading is still carried on in defiance of the law, but the provisions making the mere discovery of the bar-door open a punishable offence and entailing the forfeiture of the license on a third conviction, have naturally operated in the direction of making hotel-keepers particularly careful and cautious on Sundays. The law is unquestionably evaded by back-door visits and "drinking on the sly," still the hotels are all rigorously closed to the public gaze, and Melbourne, to all outward appearance, is on Sundays one of the most decorous and orderly cities on the face of the globe. Sunday papers are prohibited by law in Melbourne, but the music-hall managers have apparently discovered a loop-hole that enables them to repeat their Saturday night programmes on Sunday evenings by merely changing the title of the entertainment to "Rational Concert," or "Sacred and Classical Concert." A sacred selection or two may be thrown in to colourably comply with the law, but the comic and secular songs of the London halls are openly advertised and repeated in Melbourne on Sunday evenings. This very undesirable and, it is to be hoped, short-lived innovation is obviously a blasphemous, uncalled-for, and offensive incongruity. The wonder is that it should have been permitted even for a month in a country where the late distinguished astronomer, R. A. Proctor, was threatened with a prosecution if he dared to lecture on Sunday evening on the wonders and glories of the heavens.

Some years ago the temperance party in Melbourne boldly entered into direct and active competition with the licensed publicans, by forming limited liability companies and erecting coffee palaces in the principal thoroughfares of the city and suburbs. These institutions were intended to supply all the advantages of well-conducted hotels without any of the drawbacks, annoyances, and temptations incidental to the presence of drinking bars and the sale of intoxicants. They were in particular to protect strangers and visitors from the dangers and the pitfalls of the low-class public-houses, to which many of these classes were wont to gravitate. No expense was spared to make the city coffee palaces cheerful, comfortable, and attractive. Some of them were indeed constructed on a colossal scale, resembling huge hotels of the Metropole type, and ranking amongst the most striking of modern Melbourne structures. As is usually the case with novel institutions, they drew crowds for a time and enjoyed a few years of busy dividend-paying popularity. But business has fallen off greatly during recent years, expenses, not to mention dividends, can hardly be paid, and the discontented shareholders are clamouring for the conversion of the coffee palaces into places duly licensed to sell intoxicating drinks. They allege, what is notoriously true, that the coffee palaces are patronized to no small extent by people who purchase wines and spirits at the nearest public-house, and consume them on the premises dedicated to teetotalism, and they argue that it would be more honest as well as business-like if the Coffee Palace Companies were to accept both the responsibility and the revenue arising from this unforeseen condition of things. However that may eventuate, it must be confessed that the coffee palaces have failed to realize the high hopes and sanguine anticipations of their founders, and that temperance enthusiasts in the Colonies as well as Great Britain have not yet succceded in devising an acceptable and permanent substitute for the hotels and the drinking shops that they so energetically and persistently strive to abolish.

XXIV.

SPORT IN THE SOUTHERN HEMISPHERE.

The Australians are beyond all question the most ardent and persistent devotees of sport on the face of the globe. Their passionate attachment to all forms of open-air recreations and athletic exercises is no doubt very largely the result of exceptional climatic conditions. They dwell in a favoured land of practically perennial sunshine, and are constantly subject to the strong temptation to cast cares aside and go out of doors to enjoy God's glorious ozone. That they very cheerfully succumb to this ever-present temptation no one needs to be informed who has travelled through the Australian colonies, for the universality of horse-racing, and the conspicuous popularity of cricket, football, rowing, &c., proclaim the fact in loud and unmistakable tones. How far it is good for the new race of native Australians now springing up that sport in all its varieties should hold the first place in their affections, is a question to which the parliamentary adjective "contentious" might not unreasonably be prefixed. The prevailing colonial view would probably be that a fine healthy, well-disciplined, muscular race was in process of development, under the formative influence of manly sports continuously practised under a genial sky, while the observant stranger would doubtless arrive at the conclusion that brain would inevitably suffer from this constant cultivation of muscle, that great cricketers and footballers would be produced at the expense of the higher and more intellectual pursuits of life, and that the national character of the Australian branch of the British race would not be improved by the subordination of mental to physical ideals of culture and pre-eminence. Which of these judgments approaches the more nearly to correctness the early future will determine, but in the meantime I may record, as a matter of personal experience and observation, that the domination of sport in Australia was never more supreme and all-embracing than during my recent visit. With the arrival of Mr. Stoddart and his brilliant array of performers with bat and ball, cricket was unanimously elevated to the highest pedestal of public idolatry. From one end of Australia to the other nothing was talked about but the results of recently decided test matches, and anticipations of similar contests yet to be determined. Enormous crowds assembled in Sydney, Melbourne, and Adelaide, and paid for admission to the space around the arena in which the chosen representatives of the old land and the new contested for the cricketing supremacy. When Adelaide was the scene of battle, thousands hung around the newspaper offices of Melbourne and Sydney for the whole of the afternoon, and watched the posting-up of the telegrams announcing the incidents and vicissitudes of the game with vastly more interest and curiosity then they would have displayed in the outburst and progress of a European revolution. The evening papers came out in rapid editions, with detailed reports of the varying fortunes of the game, and were bought up as fast as the runners could take the money. Obviously cricket has effected a firm hold on the favour and imagination of Australians of all classes and conditions of life, and the likelihood of the daughter-land at the Antipodes establishing a permanent supremacy over the mother-country in the playing of the national game is by no means such a remote contingency as it may at first sight appear. Judging from the immense amount of cricketing and cricketing practice that is going on every afternoon in the numerous parks and open spaces of Sydney, Melbourne, and other large colonial centres, a generation of performers with bat and ball is growing up on Australian soil that will eclipse anything and everything hitherto recorded in cricketing annals. And the colonial cricketer enjoys an enormous advantage over his British brother in the facilities the Australian climate affords for playing and practising almost the whole year round. In the middle of the year there is a sort of cricketing recess, during which football has an innings and draws equally enthusiastic crowds to the parks and reserves, but there is no such climatic necessity for the cessation of cricket in Australia as operates in England, to prevent the playing of the national game for six months out of the twelve.

Every town, every village in Australia rejoices in a local racecourse and its "great annual race-meeting." Each district has its own appointed racing holidays, and all districts contribute to swell the concourse of racing pilgrims that travel to Melbourne to assist at the renowned sporting carnival of the Southern Hemisphere, which is known all over the continent as the "Cup."

During the first week of November Melbourne is taxed to its utmost capacity to accommodate the strangers within the gates. Government House, the baronial pile on the southern side of the Yarra, in which the Queen's representative is housed, is turned for the nonce into a caravansary for the benefit of the visiting Viceroys of the other Colonies, their wives and their families. By a curious coincidence, all Her Majesty's ships in the South Pacific invariably find themselves securely anchored in the harbour of Melbourne when "Cup

Week" comes round—a fortunate accident that enables the officers to mingle in the vice-regal festivities and display their uniforms to the admiring throng on the racecourse. Flemington, the course on which the race for the "Cup" is annually decided, is a perfectly level basin, a little to the west of the city, admirably adapted by nature to the purpose to which it has been applied by sport-loving man, and commanded by a serviceable eminence from whose summit the great bulk of the spectators can follow the race from start to finish. The Victoria Racing Club, the body that exercises a jurisdiction in Australia akin to that of the Jockey Club at home, is constantly improving on the natural advantages of the spot and beautifying it with all the resources of art, culture, and good taste, so much so that Lord Rosebery's epigrammatic summary of the Melbourne Cup he witnessed, "a garden-party with a race thrown in," by no means errs, as some epigrams do, in the direction of sacrificing truth to picturesque and pointed expression. Indeed, the sly suggestiveness of Lord Rosebery's observation, that the "Cup" ranks as high in the category of society functions as in that of great racing carnivals, is becoming more apparent and more emphasized with each succeeding year. Every colonial lady who is within the charmed circle of Antipodean society, or who is ambitious of entering therein, pays particular attention and attaches the highest importance to her "Cup Dress," for she knows that the newspapers devote as much, if not more, space to the description of the dresses, as they do to the account of the great race itself. Notwithstanding the severity of the financial crisis, and the universality of the business depression in the Colonies, there was no great falling off last "Cup Day," either in the brilliancy of the ladies' toilets or the denseness of the cosmopolitan crowd. The fact that one sweep promoter alone was entrusted with no less than £300,000 by the confiding public in connection with the race for the "Cup," points to the conclusion that there is still a fair amount of loose cash in the Colonies, and also affords a significant index to the strength and prevalence of the gambling spirit. It is unfortunately only too true that the Melbourne Cup is every year made the excuse and the occasion for an appalling amount of reckless betting and venturing amongst old and young, especially the latter. In the Colonies, no less than in the mother country, the general addiction of the rising generation to gambling and speculating on horse-races is a very unsatisfactory and disquieting sign of the times. For months before the "Cup" has been contested and decided, the chances of possible winners constitute the main object of interest and the leading topic of conversation amongst hundreds of thousands of the inhabitants of Greater Britain. It is as a grand national outing, the recognized gathering-ground of colonial cousins, the most likely meeting-place of old and scattered acquaintances, the converging centre of an enormous but good-tempered and well-ordered colonial assemblage, a favourable opportunity for organizing a beauty-show under interesting and attractive conditions—it is under such social aspects as these that the Melbourne Cup can be most cheerfully and satisfactorily contemplated.

XXV.

A COUPLE OF GOLDEN CITIES.

BALLARAT, where Mr. Stoddart and his triumphant team of English cricketers were, at the time of my visit, displaying their prowess with bat and ball, is the most pleasing and picturesque of Australian goldfields, but Anthony Trollope's description of it as the " most beautiful of Colonial cities" is, perhaps, a little too eulogistic for general acceptance. The fact is that, by some wise provision of nature, golden deposits are usually found beneath dreary and desolate tracts of country; so it is quite refreshing to find one's self in a golden city like Ballarat, that combines a choice array of surrounding scenery with the possession of mineral wealth. A considerable number of statues have been erected in the principal thoroughfare of Ballarat—Sturt Street—since my last visit. Robert Burns and Thomas Moore, the national bards of Scotland and Ireland, are conspicuous, and Shakspeare would be keeping them company now but for the banking crisis of 1893. The funds subscribed for the statue of Shakspeare had the misfortune to be placed in one of the suspended banks, and are now locked up, and will not be available for some time to come. The newest and most interesting of the Ballarat statues is the heroic bronze figure of the Hon. Peter Lalor, late Speaker of the Victorian Parliament. It is the work of a London sculptor, Mr. T. Nelson Maclean, who is to be complimented on the remarkable fidelity of the likeness and the striking impressiveness of the figure. Mr. Lalor, the son of the then Member for the Queen's County in the House of Commons, was one of the pioneer gold-diggers at Ballarat, and by his oratorical powers and force of character, he soon acquired a commanding influence in the ranks of the miners. The obnoxious license-fee imposed on all diggers alike, whether successful or unsuccessful, and collected in a brutal and truculent fashion by a police largely recruited from the ranks of transported convicts, finally drove the digging population of Ballarat into open and undisguised rebellion. Lalor was unanimously chosen as commander-in-chief of the rebel diggers, who entrenched themselves within a stockade, which was attacked and stormed one Sunday morning by an Imperial force, under the command of Colonel Thomas. Lalor was amongst the wounded, and had an arm amputated. He was carried away by his retreating comrades to a place of safety, where he remained for some weeks a fugitive, with a high price on his head. Proclamations offered handsome rewards to anybody who would bring him in, dead or alive; but, although his hiding-place was known to hundreds, no one could be found to betray him.

Soon after the rebellion Parliamentary representation was conferred upon the diggers, and Lalor came forth from his retirement to become the first member for Ballarat, amid a scene of popular enthusiasm. The detested license-fee was speedily abolished, an export duty on gold being substituted in its stead, so that, although the diggers' revolt was stamped out by the armed forces of the Crown, the principles for which they took up arms really triumphed and became the law of the land. Ever since that unhappy collision between the Crown and the mining population, Ballarat has been one of the most peaceable, prosperous, and progressive cities in the British Empire. The Hon. Duncan Gillies, who now represents Victoria in London, was also a pioneer gold-digger at Ballarat, and worked for some time in the same claim with Lalor, so that it was only right and proper that he should unveil the statue of his old "mate," which he did after a graceful and interesting speech. Mr. Gillies held aloof from Lalor's insurrectionary movement, and thereby incurred some temporary unpopularity, but he lived it down, succeeded in becoming the miners' representative on the bench of the local

Court, and from that vantage-ground vaulted into Parliament as member for Ballarat West.

Ballarat is a bishopric of both the Catholic and Anglican denominations. Dr. Samuel Thornton, the Anglican prelate, is the son of a member of the staff of *The Times*, and was, in the early years of his clerical career, a very active and aggressive missionary in the East-end of London. His energy and aggressiveness may be gauged by the fact that he was twice taken into custody by the police for obstructing the thoroughfare in the Mile End Road by his vigorous open-air preaching. He has not come into personal collision with the authorities during his twenty years' residence in Ballarat, but he is still a very pugnacious and uncompromising speaker, who does not hesitate to say in honest Saxon what he thinks, or to hold up his end of the argument throughout the resultant controversies. He was curate of St. Jude's, Whitechapel, and rector of St. George's, Birmingham, before he was chosen as the first Anglican Bishop of Ballarat. During my stay he had as his guest the Right Rev. Dr. Wordsworth, Bishop of Salisbury, who recently made an extensive tour of the Colonies. Dr. Wordsworth, dressed in rough miners' clothes, descended one of the deepest of Ballarat gold mines, and saw for himself the whole process of extracting the auriferous quartz from the bowels of the earth. The late Duke of Clarence and the present Duke of York had a similar educational experience in Ballarat when their Royal Highnesses visited Victoria as midshipmen on board the *Bacchante*. Ballarat has had many distinguished guests during the forty-four years of its existence, and its history as narrated by **Mr. W. B.** Withers, a veteran member of the local press, in a handsome illustrated volume, furnishes very interesting and romantic reading. The ups **and** downs of digging life, the strange vicissitudes of gold mines, the varying, but strongly-marked, types of character on the goldfields, suggest a field of fiction that has so far been only superficially scratched by the pen of the novelist.

Unlike Ballarat, Bendigo is to be ranked **with** the generality of goldfields, as a dusty, arid-looking, unpicturesque, and **not** particularly inviting sort of place from the standpoint of the casual tourist. All its loveliness and interest are subterranean, for Bendigo is now proved to be a series of goldfields, one underneath the other. How far downwards they extend nobody **can** tell. The Bendigo gold mines are now the deepest in the world, and the signs of exhaustion of the auriferous quartz are not yet apparent. I found hardly any perceptible change in Bendigo after several years' absence. **At** the time of my visit old Bendigonians were rejoicing over the honour conferred on one of their number, the Hon. John McIntyre, M.P., by the Queen. Quite unexpectedly Mr. McIntyre's name **figured in** the list of New **Year** knights. He was a fiery Radical in the early fifties, and once declared his willingness to lead the Bendigo diggers in a march and attack on Melbourne. He was the leading spirit in the "Red Ribbon League," an organized body of Bendigo diggers determined to have their grievances redressed. At Bendigo wiser counsels prevailed than at Ballarat, and there was no hostile collision between the military and the digging population, although the situation was very critical and menacing there during the period that the Ballarat diggers were up in arms. When the grievances of the diggers were constitutionally redressed, Mr. McIntyre gradually drifted away from Radicalism, became Conservative in his political tastes, and is now one of the recognized chiefs of the Constitutional Party. There seems something paradoxical about the knighting of a champion of Conservatism by an Imperial Radical Government. If Lord Salisbury had knighted Mr. McIntyre, it would have been perfectly natural, seeing that Lord Salisbury is himself an old Bendigonian. He spent some time on this goldfield in 1852, as Lord Robert Cecil, and a number of questionable traditions concerning him are current amongst the surviving pioneers. Whether Bendigo owes its name to the famous English pugilist of that style and title, or whether it is a corruption of a local aboriginal word, is a question that has not yet been definitely decided.

XXVI.

AUSTRALIAN FACTS AND PROSPECTS.

THE latest work of the genial, observant, and philosophical Anglo-Frenchman, who writes under the pseudonym of Max O'Rell, deals largely with his impressions and experiences of the Australian colonies, in which, for close on two years, he lectured to large and appreciative audiences. In some of his judgments there is a combination of characteristic shrewdness, playful satire, keen penetration, and intelligent insight, whilst in others the hasty, unverified, and ill-digested conclusions of the rapid and rushing note-taker are but too apparent. His strictures on the condition of morality in Sydney have given no little offence in that city, and have been resented with indignation in the columns of the local press. While Max O'Rell has certainly somewhat over-coloured this particular picture, it must at the same time be acknowledged that there are sights and scenes in Sydney of a very repulsive and demoralizing character. One crying iniquity in particular ought to be removed by legislation as speedily as possible, and that is the system of subletting rooms in hotels for the purpose of conversion into what are called "private bars." No other city in the British Empire sanctions such a pestiferous practice as this. These private bars are rented out by the licensee to young female decoys, who pay as high as 16*l*. per week for the accommodation. It is not by the sale of liquor that they recoup themselves, but by converting the private bar into a place of assignation and a mart of vice. These private bars are nightly frequented by numbers of young men, with results that may be easily imagined. They are not obtruded on the gaze of the ordinary visitor. They minister to the illicit requirements of a special class, who know by experience which curtain to push aside in order that a particular private bar, its presiding divinity, and her attendant satellites, may be revealed. This scandalous state of things may be permissible under the present licensing law, but, if so, the sooner an amending Act is passed, the better for the moral elevation and the good repute of the city of Sydney.

Drunkenness is described by Max O'Rell as the "national vice in the Colonies," and he attributes its prevalence to the absence of social, artistic, and intellectual distractions. The habit of drinking is certainly more conspicuous in the Colonies than elsewhere. There is a greater publicity about it, a gratuitous contempt for anything in the nature of concealment or reticence, that is a traditional survival of the rollicking, free-and-easy days of the goldfields, the flush times of the fifties and sixties, when universal drinking was the rule and practice, and a refusal to join the convivial circle was resented by the lucky digger as a gross personal affront, almost justifying the use of the revolver on the spot. This baneful custom of "shouting," or insisting on everyone present drinking with the hospitable individual who issues the invitation, is still a colonial institution in a certain sense, but it is visibly declining and becoming less in vogue every year, as it is entirely out of harmony with the tastes and sympathies of the rising race of native Australians. In England and on the Continent Australian wines are annually increasing in popularity, thanks to the enterprise and perseverance of Mr. P. B. Burgoyne, but in Australia itself they are far from being regarded with general favour—a want of appreciation that is much to be regretted, as the colonial population would undoubtedly be more temperate as a whole if the local wines were locally consumed on a larger scale than at present. As for the absence of social, artistic, and intellectual recreations, which in Max O'Rell's opinion drives colonists to over-indulgence in intoxicants, that allegation may apply to the idle and ignorant rich, who unfortunately constitute no inconsiderable proportion of the colonial wealthy classes, but it is certainly not true of the great bulk of the community. Wealth, in too many instances, falls into the hands of colonists who are utterly destitute of the capacity to turn it to proper account. Suddenly-enriched speculators, who take no thought of public duty or of benefiting their less fortunate fellows, who recognize no social obligations or responsibilities, who are absolutely indifferent to the merits of the finest picture or statue, and who find it an impossibility to interest themselves in the perusal of an elevating and informing book— such as these naturally and steadily gravitate towards the whisky-jar and the brandy-bottle, and it is from this comparatively small but unduly conspicuous class that Max O'Rell's shocking examples have been drawn.

In connection with Max O'Rell's statement that already people in Australia are beginning to boast of not working with their hands, who have inherited fortunes earned by means of hard work and a life of complete abnegation, it is worthy of note that the recent financial crisis has brought out in a striking manner the energy, independence, and self-reliance of the cultured daughters of Australia. A number of high and prosperous families were suddenly reduced from affluence to penury by the failure of the banks and kindred institutions, but the young ladies of these devastated households, reared in the lap of ease and luxury, and believing themselves secure in the possession of thousands of pounds, boldly faced the swiftly and sadly altered circumstances, adapted themselves to their changed condition of life, went into business in Melbourne, opened refreshment rooms and shops of various descriptions, and are now earning a livelihood for themselves and those dependent on them by the exercise of their own industry, ability, and resolute determination not to succumb to the slings and arrows of outrageous fortune.

Max O'Rell alleges that the adoration of the golden calf is more noticeable in the Colonies than in England, but that, unfortunately, is the characteristic vice of all young and suddenly-enriched communities. It is only when such heterogeneous masses of humanity consolidate and settle down into the quiet and regular grooves of the well-ordered State, that respect for literature, science, art, and intellectual achievements generally, challenges the all-pervading worship of wealth, and succeeds in reducing the erstwhile omnipotent money-raker to a lower pedestal. The Colonies have not yet arrived at this desirable stage of development, and whatever there is in them of literary, artistic, and scientific excellence has to go to England for effectual recognition, encouragement, and support. Wealth is still the only acknowledged criterion of success, and practically the only passport to the sacred precincts of Government House. It might reasonably be expected that the representatives of Her Majesty, men who had breathed for most of their lives the higher old-world atmosphere of culture, taste, and refinement, would rise superior to the gold-bag ideal of human greatness, but the average Governor unfortunately only too readily drops down to the level that he finds on landing and remains there, making the possession of wealth the principal if not the sole qualification for vice-regal hospitality. Governors could do much to elevate the standard of colonial ideals, and it is to be regretted that they so frequently fail to rise to the height of their opportunities.

Max O'Rell pronounces a very hasty and ill-informed judgment when he sums up the Australian working-man as "lazy, fond of drink, a devoted keeper of St. Monday, a spendthrift, who thinks only of his pleasures, and takes no interest whatever in the development of his country." Some there may be, who correspond to this unflattering description, but the typical Australian working-man is something far different—shrewd, energetic, temperate, thrifty, and keenly and intelligently interested in public affairs. The critic-lecturer is on safer ground when he deplores the hostile attitude of the colonial workers towards immigration from the old land. They object to immigration because they believe it will have the effect of reducing the standard of wages, but that is a wholly fallacious assumption. Australia ought to be peopled by forty millions instead of four, as her permanent prosperity largely depends on the filling-up of the vast unoccupied spaces on her map, and the consequent development of her boundless and varied resources. None would benefit more than the working-classes themselves from the steady and systematic pursuance of such an enlightened, practical, and far-seeing policy.

Australian working-men would also do well to moderate the transports of their ardour for Protection. Every young country naturally has a preference for Protection, with a view to fostering and developing its native industries, until they are able to stand alone and compete on fair and equitable terms with the long-established industries of older lands. Such a policy is a wise and prudent one, when kept within reasonable bounds, but when it is allowed to run riot and ride roughshod over every other interest, it approximates more closely to a curse than a blessing. Melbourne is a shocking example of Protection run mad. Duties were piled up to such prohibitive altitudes by the protectionist Parliamentary majority, that the ships which formerly abounded in the harbour of Melbourne were driven away to the rival metropolis, Sydney, and the commerce of Melbourne has sustained a shock from which it will take some time to recover. Moreover, the artificial inducements offered by the State-subsidized industries drained the provincial towns and districts of a large amount of their life-blood, so much so, that at one time Melbourne actually had almost one-half of the population of the colony within its metropolitan radius. It was this abnormal and feverish state of things that paved the way for the mischievous madness of the land-boom era. Fortunately, a strong reaction against these extravagant and far-fetched theories of Protection has set in, and the Parliament sitting in Melbourne is now engaged on the salutary work of cutting down duties to reasonable and legitimate lengths. Moderation, not only in the matter of Protection, but also in the conduct of the numerous experiments in State socialism on which several of the colonies have light-heartedly embarked, must be the watchword of the future. Australia has been frequently described in the London Press as "the laboratory of the Empire," but the practical consideration for Australians is that care, caution, and consistent sanity are more necessary in a laboratory than anywhere else, if disastrous explosions and other unpleasant possibilities are to be averted. Possessing a magnificent extent of still unoccupied territory, an immensity of undeveloped wealth, a glorious climate, an active and enterprising population, and the capacity of rapid recovery from the effects of unfavourable seasons and conditions, Australia is a land of great promise and potentialities, whose history in the future will, I hope and believe, wipe out the errors of the past and be a worthy record of well-ordered progress and prosperity.

INDEX.

ABERDEEN, Earl of, 89.
Australia, Future of, 230.
Austral Salon, 174.

BALLARAT, 217.
Barnardo, Dr., 87.
Bendigo, 221.
Bent, Hon. Thomas, 162.
Berry, Sir Graham, 167.
Besant, Mrs. Annie, 138, 198.
Bevan, Rev. Dr., 183.
Blake, Hon. Edward, 75.
Boldrewood, Rolf, 165, 173.
Bowell, Sir Mackenzie, 67.
Brassey, Lord, 21, 89.
Bright, John, 125.
British Columbia, 95.
Brooke, G. V., 192.
Browning, Robert, 125.
Brownless, Sir A. C., 195.
Buxton, M.P., Mr. Sydney, 26.

CAFFYN, Mrs. Mannington, 176.
Cambridge, Ada, 176.
Canadian Pacific Railway, 43, 80, 85, 88, 94.
Carlyle, Thomas, 124.
Carr, Archbishop, 182.
Carrington, Lord, 122.
Cathcart, Mr. J. F., 145.
Childers, Right Hon. H. C. E., 196.
Chinese Question, 95.

Clarke, Sir Andrew, 21.
Clarke, Marcus, 174.
Cleveland, President, 100.
Cobden, Richard, 125.
Coffee Palaces, 208.
Cole's Book Arcade, 176.
Colmer, Mr. J. G., 35.
Colonial Cricket, 211.
Coppin, Hon. George, 147, 190.
Costigan, Hon. John, 69.
Cup Festival, Melbourne, 213.
Curran, Hon. J. J., 42, 69.

DAVIES, Sir M. H., 158.
Deakin, Hon. Alfred, 168.
Dibbs, Sir George, 8, 128.
Duffy, Sir C. G., 21, 126, 197.
Duffy, Hon. J. G., 170.

FEDERATION, 29, 130.
Fiji, 24, 106.
Fitzgibbon, Mr. E. G., 201.

GEELONG, 23.
Gillies, Hon. Duncan, 219.
Gladstone, Right Hon. W. E., 10, 61, 124.
Goe, Bishop, 182.
Grant, General, 125.
Greenway, Hon. Thomas, 82.
Grey Nunnery, 47.

HARRIS, Sir Augustus, 143.

INDEX.

Hawaii, 98.
Higinbotham, Hon. George, 21, 162.
Honolulu, 102.
Horne, R. H., 172, 200.
Huddart, Mr. James, 2, 32, 34, 67, 83.

RVING, Sir Henry, 143.

JERSEY, Earl of, 2, 68.

KANAKA TRAFFIC, 29.
Kean, Charles, 146, **189**, 193.
Keeley, Mrs., 148.
Kimberley, Lord, 131.
Kingsley, Henry, 173.
Kipling, Rudyard, 175.
Kirkpatrick, Colonel, **74**.

LABOUR PARTY, 170.
Lalor, Hon. Peter, 21, **218**.
Land-booming, 153, 205.
Laurier, Hon. Wilfrid, 96.
Local Option, 22, 206.
Longfellow, H. W., 125.
Lorne, Marquis of, 80.
Lowe, Robert, 9, **123**, 197.

MACARTNEY, Dean, 180.
Macdonald, Sir John, 65, 93.
Manitoba, 84.
Manning, Sir W. P., 7.
Martin, Lady Theodore, **149**.
McCulloch, Sir James, 21.
McGee, Hon. Thos. D'Arcy, 42.
McIntyre, Sir John, 221.
McNeil, Rev. John, 135.
Melbourne, **14**, 150.
Michie, Sir Archibald, 21, **196**.
Mill, J. S., 125.
Montreal, **38**.
Moorhouse, Bishop, 181.
Moran, Cardinal, **12**, 139.
Morley, Right Hon. John, 84.

Mowatt, Sir Oliver, 74.
Munro, Hon. James, 160.

NEILD, Dr. J. E., 199.

O'CONNELL, Daniel, 124.
O'Rell, Max, 117, 198, 223.
O'Shanassy, Sir John, 21.
Ottawa, 59.

PARKES, Sir Henry, 8, 119.
Patterson, Sir J. B., 20.
Private Bars, 224.
Protection, 229.

QUEBEC, 36.

REGINA, 90.
Reid, Hon. G. H., 8, 11, 133.
Rignold, Mr. George, 143.
Rocky Mountains, 92.
Rosebery, Lord, 7, 113, 121, 131, 214.

SALA, Mr. George Augustus, 152, 198.
Salisbury, Marquis of, 222.
Schultz, Governor, 81.
Selwyn, Dr., 62.
Shaughnessy, Mr. T. G., 45.
Sisters of St. Joseph, 49.
Smith, Sir Frank, 75.
Smith, James, 200.
Smith, Murray, 167.
Smythe, R. S., 198.
Spiers and Pond, 179.
Spiritualism, 137.
Stanmore, Lord, 110.
State Socialism, 230.
Stawell, Sir William, 21.
Stevenson, Robert Louis, **175**.
Strong, Rev. Charles, 184.
Sullivan, Barry, 189.
Sydney, 6, 112.

"TASMA," 176.

Thompson, Sir John, 63.
Thornton, Bishop, 220.
Thurston, Sir J. B., 25, 109.
Toronto, 71.
Trades' Hall, 203.
Turner, Hon. G., 20, 169.

VANCOUVER, 5, 95.

Van Horne, Sir William, 44.
Verdon, Sir George, 21.

WALLACE, Hon. N. C., 69.
Whitehead, Charles, 172, 200.
Williamson, Mr. J. C., 189.
Winnipeg, **4,** 78.
Wolseley, Lord, **4, 77.**

ADVERTISEMENTS. v

The Best is the Cheapest!
Fixed, moderate prices
For first Quality.

JAEGER.

PURE WOOL UNDERWEAR, HOSIERY, PYJAMAS, RUGS, BLANKETS, DRESSING GOWNS, SHAWLS, CORSETS, BOOTS AND SHOES, &c., &c.

TRADE MARK. Permanent Protection from Chill.
Dr. Jaeger's HEALTH CULTURE, 188 pp., and the Jaeger Co.'s Catalogue, post free. Depôts in many Colonies and Towns. Address sent by

Dr. JAEGER'S SANITARY WOOLLEN SYSTEM CO., Ltd.
Wholesale and Shipping Warehouse,
95, Milton Street, London, E.C.
Australian Branch,
41, York Street, Sydney, N.S.W.;
314, Flinders Lane, Melbourne, Vic.

ON EACH GARMENT.

LIPTON'S TEAS.

FINEST THE WORLD CAN PRODUCE.	Tea Merchant BY SPECIAL APPOINTMENT TO HER MAJESTY, THE QUEEN.	RICH, PURE, AND FRAGRANT.
Per 1/7 lb.		Per 1/- & 1/4 lb.

LARGEST SALE IN THE WORLD.

LIPTON, Tea, Coffee, & Cocoa Planter, CEYLON.

AUSTRALIA, HONOLULU, FIJI, NEW ZEALAND.

NEW SWIFT PASSENGER ROUTE by Swiftest Atlantic Steamers (any Line) to Montreal, Boston, or New York; thence *via*

CANADIAN PACIFIC RAILWAY AND VANCOUVER,

Taking in the Grand Scenery of the "Rockies." ONLY ACTUAL TRANS-CONTINENTAL LINE RUNNING THROUGH TRAINS UNDER ONE MANAGEMENT—ATLANTIC TO PACIFIC. Many optional Routes, including Niagara and Chicago. Break of Journey allowed.

STEAMSHIPS OF THE
CANADIAN-AUSTRALIAN LINE
Sail Monthly.

LARGEST, SWIFTEST, and FINEST RUNNING FROM AMERICAN CONTINENT to AUSTRALASIA.

Calling at
VICTORIA, B.C., HONOLULU, FIJI, AND SYDNEY.

Electric Light, Hot and Cold Baths, Good Cuisine, Exceptionally Large Cabins. For descriptive Pamphlets, Tickets, and Berths, apply to Passenger Department, CANADIAN PACIFIC RAILWAY, 67, King William Street, London, E.C., or to The Managing Owner, JAMES HUDDART, 22, Billiter Street, London, E.C.; and in Australasia, to HUDDART, PARKER & CO., LTD., Chief Offices, Sydney, Melbourne, and Wellington. Agencies in various Australasian ports.

P. AND O.
MAIL STEAMERS
FROM LONDON TO

BOMBAY, GIBRALTAR, MALTA, BRINDISI, EGYPT, ADEN, and MADRAS, *via* BOMBAY } Every week.

CALCUTTA, COLOMBO, CHINA, STRAITS, JAPAN, AUSTRALIA, NEW ZEALAND, TASMANIA } Every fortnight.

CHEAP RETURN TICKETS.

For particulars, apply at the Company's Offices, 122, Leadenhall Street, London, E.C., and 25, Cockspur Street, London, S.W.

Works by J. F. Hogan, M.P.

The Irish in Australia.
Crown 8vo, 2s. 6d.

"An excellent contribution to the literature of the great Irish question."—THE EARL OF ABERDEEN.

"In Mr. Hogan the labours and fortunes of Ireland in Australasia have found a very pleasant and sympathetic narrator."—*Pall Mall Gazette.*

The Lost Explorer.
A STORY OF AUSTRALIAN ADVENTURE.
Price 3s. 6d.

"A very interesting work. I rely on the aboriginal manners and feats of Uralla as taken from the life."—RIGHT HON. W. E. GLADSTONE.

"The Rider Haggard of Australia. A wonderful story. Will delight boys quite as much as *Allan Quatermain* or *Kidnapped.*"—*Academy.*

The Convict King.
Price 2s. 6d.

"Not for many a long day has there been published so interesting a romance of real life. Mr. Hogan's book positively whets the reader's appetite. Like Oliver Twist, we ask for more about this marvellous man."—London *Daily Telegraph.*

THE AUSTRALIAN IN LONDON.

Crown 8vo, 6s.

" Bright and sparkling."—*Morning Post.*

"Written with much spirit and sympathy."—*Daily News.*

ROBERT LOWE, VISCOUNT SHERBROOKE.

Crown 8vo, cloth, 10s. 6d.

" Mr. Hogan has really rendered a great service to history and biography, by his account of the very remarkable part played by Mr. Lowe in his colonial career."—Mr. Justin McCarthy, M.P., in the *Pall Mall Gazette.*

" Mr. Hogan's biography of Robert Lowe is a graphic piece of literary portraiture, specially interesting because it lifts the veil which up to now has shrouded his Australian career."—London *Daily Chronicle.*

WARD AND DOWNEY
LIMITED

12 YORK BUILDINGS ADELPHI LONDON.

FREE GRANTS OF LAND IN CANADA.

See the Reports of the twelve British Tenant-Farmers who visited the Dominion in 1893.

160 Acres in Manitoba and the North-West Territories; 100 to 200 in other Provinces.

OPENINGS FOR THE INVESTMENT OF CAPITAL IN MANUFACTURES, ETC.

Improved Farms at Reasonable Prices in Nova Scotia, New Brunswick, Prince Edward Island, Quebec, Ontario, Manitoba, the North-West Territories, and British Columbia.

Tenant-Farmers and others wishing to engage in Agriculture will find many opportunities for the investment of their capital in Canada; and there is also a demand for Farm Labourers and Female Domestic Servants of Good Character.

The Reports of the Tenant-Farmer Delegates, those of Professor Long and Professor Wallace, and other Pamphlets, containing full information respecting trade and commerce, the investment of capital, land regulations, demand for labour, rates of wages, cost of living, &c., can be had on application to the Office of the High Commissioner for Canada, 17, Victoria Street, S.W. (Mr. J. G. COLMER, Secretary); or to Mr. JOHN DYKE, Canadian Government Agent, 15, Water Street, Liverpool. Information respecting the import and export trade of Canada can also be obtained from these offices.

BRITISH COLUMBIA.

ALL information respecting this Province, its climate, coal and precious metals, fisheries, timber, agriculture, fruit, hops, and other resources, may be obtained at the Office of the Agent-General in London, 39, Victoria Street, Westminster, S.W.

TALES OF CRIME AND CRIMINALS IN AUSTRALIA.
By H. A. WHITE.
Price - - - - - 6s.

"An interesting study of one of the darkest chapters of modern history. . . . Many and varied are the stories recounted in this collection."—*Publishers' Circular.*

"The very simplicity with which many of the most exciting episodes in the old days of stockades are told, gives them a force often lacking in the work of the romancer. The Story of the Kelly gang has never been set out with more effect."—*Daily Chronicle.*

WARD & DOWNEY, Ltd., 12, YORK BUILDINGS, ADELPHI.

ADVERTISEMENTS.

C. S. SWAN & HUNTER, LTD.,
Ship Builders and Repairers,
WALLSEND-ON-TYNE,
ENGLAND.

BUILDERS OF THE STEAMERS—
"New Amsterdam," "Horatia," "Essequebo,"
"Fifeshire," "Elginshire," "Courier,"
"Chancellor," "Musician," "Warrimoo,"
"Miowera," "Tasmania," "Westmeath,"
"Maori," "Aotea," "Tokomaru,"
AND OTHER WELL-KNOWN COLONIAL TRADERS.

Telegrams "HUNTER, WALLSEND."

BURGOYNE'S AUSTRALIAN WINES.

Of every Wine Merchant and Grocer in the Kingdom.

E. W. COLE

BOOKSELLER, PUBLISHER, & STATIONER,

The Book Arcade, Bourke St., Melbourne;

333, George St., Sydney ; 67, Rundle St., Adelaide.

Write or Call for any Book you want.

Periodicals and Stationery Supplied.

COLE'S BOOK-BUYERS' GUIDE AND MAGAZINE OF CHOICE EXTRACTS, New Series, Monthly, post free.

The most exhaustive Guide Published in Australasia.

WRITE FOR A COPY.

GOSSIP OF THE CENTURY.

PERSONAL AND TRADITIONAL MEMORIES — SOCIAL, LITERARY, ARTISTIC, &c.

By the Author of "Flemish Interiors," &c., 2 vols., royal 8vo, cloth, containing 1126 pages and over 100 portraits, &c. Price 42s.

"The book is far too readable to be found much fault with. It is better conceived and better written than nine-tenths of its class. . . . It starts with a budget of 'Court Gossip,' chiefly about George IV. and William IV. and their surroundings. To this follows half a volume about social, literary, and political celebrities, and after that we have chapters on soldiers, lawyers, and doctors. The second volume is filled with reminiscences of musicians, singers, actors, and public entertainers in general, painters and sculptors being included in the category. . . . More than a hundred illustrations, most of them portraits and copies of old works, add much to the interest of these sumptuous volumes."—*The Athenæum.*

"In these two large and beautifully-printed volumes we have a great amount of the century's best gossip—that kind of it which historical stocktakers of the future will ransack, not without feelings of pleasure, when they try to form some coherent idea of what we and our fathers and grandfathers of the transitional age were like, inwardly and outwardly. At the same time it is full of living interest to us of the present. . . . The two volumes are, in fact, a kind of encyclopædia of gossip about monarchs, statesmen, doctors, writers, actors, singers, soldiers, men of fashion."—*The Daily News.*

"Covering so wide a range, they (the volumes) should be of great value to the student of manners in the earlier half of the present century, the more as the old order is so rapidly changing."—*The Standard.*

WARD & DOWNEY, Ltd., 12, York Buildings, Adelphi, W.C.

FROM WARD & DOWNEY'S LIST.

By Permission of the Bishop of London.

A REPRODUCTION IN FACSIMILE OF THE ORIGINAL MANUSCRIPT HISTORY OF THE VOYAGE OF THE PILGRIM FATHERS IN THE "MAYFLOWER" AND THE FOUNDATION OF THE PLIMOTH PLANTATION. Written by WILLIAM BRADFORD, second Governor of the Colony, and now in the Library of Fulham Palace. With an Introduction by JOHN A. DOYLE, Fellow of All Souls College, Oxford. Super royal quarto, printed on hand-made paper, price £4 4s. nett.

IN A WALLED GARDEN. By Madame BESSIE RAYNER BELLOC. 1 Vol., crown 8vo, art linen, price 6s.

CONTENTS: Dorothea Casaubon and George Eliot—Joseph Priestly in Domestic Life—In Rome with Mrs. Jameson—Mary Howitt—Lady Georgiana Fullerton—An Old World Prince—Montagus and Procters—A Chapter of War —Dr. Manning of Bayswater—Catherine Booth—Comte Adolphe de Circourt —Mademoiselle Adelaide de Montgolfier, &c., &c.

SOME CELEBRATED IRISH BEAUTIES OF THE LAST CENTURY. By FRANCES GERARD, Author of "Angelica Kauffmann." With numerous Portraits and Illustrations. 1 Vol., demy 8vo, 21s.

"When true stories of a past time are told by one who can set them forth in all the grace of a good literary style, they are imbued with a finer charm than any romance. These stories possess that charm in a remarkable degree."—*Academy.*

"I well remember the interest and pleasure with which I read your Biography of the Excellent Angelica Kauffmann, and I am receiving a somewhat similar enjoyment in the perusal of your 'Irish Beauties.'"—From a letter to the Author written by the Rt. Hon. W. E. GLADSTONE.

STUDIES OF CONTEMPORARY SUPERSTITION. By W. H. MALLOCK, Author of "The New Republic," &c. 1 Vol., crown 8vo, buckram, 6s.

"A brilliant attempt to combat the Agnosticism of the day with its own weapons."—*Times.*

"It deals, with all the force and cleverness which mark Mr. Mallock's work, with some aspects of the great questions, religious and social, which occupy so much space in contemporary thought."—*Spectator.*

HERE, THERE, AND EVERYWHERE. By BARON DE MALORTIE, Author of "Twixt Old Times and New." 1 Vol., demy 8vo, 15s.

"It is a lively collection of personal recollections and sketches of contemporary personages."—*Times.*

"A most entertaining and readable book."—*Spectator.*

LIVINGSTONE IN AFRICA. By the late Hon. RODEN NOEL. Now ready. With Critical Introduction by Miss E. HICKEY, and 20 Illustrations by Hume Nisbet. 1 Vol., pott 4to, price 10s. 6d.

NEW NOVELS.

JACOB NIEMAND. By ROBERT H. SHERARD. 1 Vol., crown 8vo, cloth, price 6s.

"The story is essentially pathetic, but it is seldom lacking in animation, and there is abundance of light comedy to relieve the gravity."—*The Times.*

"There is not a page that drags. It is a good story from start to finish."—*The Queen.*

NEW NOVELS—continued.

FELIX DORRIEN: a Novel. By R. LUCAS. With Illustrations by the Lady Boston. 1 Vol., crown 8vo, cloth extra, price 6s.

HIS LAST CARD: a new Novel by KATHERINE S. MACQUOID, Author of "At an Old Chateau," &c. 1 Vol., crown 8vo, cloth extra, price 6s.

A DAUGHTER OF THE MARIONIS. By E. PHILLIPS OPPENHEIM. 1 Vol., crown 8vo, cloth extra, price 6s.
"As a story pure and simple, we have read few books for a long time to be compared with it."—*Weekly Sun.*

THE REAL CHARLOTTE. By E. Œ. SOMERVILLE and MARTIN ROSS. A new Edition. 1 Vol., crown 8vo, art canvas, price 6s.
"'The Real Charlotte' is perhaps one of the best modern examples of an English (or rather of an Irish) realistic novel extant."—*Pall Mall Gazette.*

EARL LAVENDER. By JOHN DAVIDSON. A Full and True Account of the Wonderful Mission of Earl Lavender, which lasted One Night and One Day. 1 Vol., crown 8vo, buckram, 6s. With a Frontispiece by Aubrey Beardsley. Second Thousand.
"An amazingly clever novel-farce."—*Queen.*

VERA BARANTZOVA. From the Russian of Sophia Kovalevsky. By S. STEPNIAK and W. WESTALL. Price 6s.
"A simple, straightforward tale of modern Nihilism."—*National Observer.*
"Of its kind it is perfect."—*Spectator.*

GIFT BOOKS FOR CHILDREN.
By THEODORA C. ELMSLIE.

THE LITTLE LADY OF LAVENDER. With Illustrations by EDITH SCANNELL and H. L. E. One Vol., imperial 16mo, cloth extra, gilt, 3s. 6d.

THOSE MIDSUMMER FAIRIES. With Illustrations by J. B. ELMSLIE and others. Crown 8vo, cloth extra, gilt top, 3s. 6d.

BLACK PUPPY: A Story for Children. With seven full page Illustrations. Imp. 16mo, cloth extra, 3s. 6d.

THE ORDEAL OF THOMAS TAFFLER, COSTERMONGER. By HENRY MURRAY, Author of "A Man of Genius," &c. With Illustrations by B. S. LE FANU. Fcap. 8vo. price 1s. 6d.

NEW NOVELS AT ONE SHILLING.
In Uniform Binding.

THE MYSTERY OF CLOOMBER. By A. CONAN DOYLE.
OLIVER'S BRIDE: A True Story. By Mrs. OLIPHANT.
THE MASTER OF THE SILVER SEA. By MORLEY ROBERTS.
THE BISHOP'S DELUSION. By ALAN ST. AUBYN.
THE CREED OF PHILIP GLYN. By the Hon. Mrs. ALAN BRODRICK.

WILLIAM WESTALL'S NOVELS.
New Issue, in handsome cloth binding, at 2s.

THE OLD FACTORY: A Lancashire Story.	NIGEL FORTESCUE; or, The Hunted Man.
RED RYVINGTON.	BIRCH DENE.
RALPH NORBRECK'S TRUST.	TWO PINCHES OF SNUFF.
HER TWO MILLIONS.	ROY OF ROY'S COURT.

WARD & DOWNEY, Ltd., 12, York Buildings, Adelphi, W.C.

THE INNS of COURT HOTEL
LIMITED.

Entrances: Holborn and Lincoln's Inn Fields, London.

A High-class Family Hotel, with 200 Bedrooms, happily situated, having all modern conveniences and a

MODERATE TARIFF.

PURE ARTESIAN WELL WATER. See Certificate.

ELECTRIC LIGHTS. LIFTS.

PERFECT SANITARY ARRANGEMENTS & FIRE PROTECTION.

Suites and Single Rooms. Masonic Lodge Rooms. Wedding Receptions, Banquets, &c., Arranged.

THE GRAND HALL

Is the finest in England. Afternoon Teas, Ices, &c., are served here.

TABLE D'HÔTE,

6 to 8, 3s. 6d., at Separate Tables (in the pleasantest room in London).

RESTAURANT

Open to Non-residents from 7 a.m. till midnight.

FRANK BLACKLEY,
Manager (late of Sydney).

TARIFF GRATIS.

CANADIAN PACIFIC RAILWAY.

The only actual Trans-Continental Railway on the American Continent. The longest Line under one Management in the World. Its Trains and Steamers extend in a direct line from Atlantic tide-water to Hong Kong, 9,180 miles.

FREE FARMS to all settlers in the Canadian North-West.

PASSENGERS from Europe, Home-seekers, Tourists and Sportsmen, leave the Trans-Atlantic Steamers at Quebec in summer, and at either Halifax, New York, or Portland (Maine), according to circumstances, during the winter months. At all of these ports they will be met by an Agent of the Company, who will take charge of them, see after baggage, and furnish all needful information concerning the journey.

JAPAN AND CHINA.—By the new British Short Route. "Empress of India," "Empress of Japan," "Empress of China," 6,000 tons gross, 10,000 h.p., fastest, finest, and only Twin-Screw Steamers on the Pacific Ocean, leave Vancouver every three weeks.

ROUND THE WORLD.—By arrangement with the P. & O. Co. and various other Lines, *viâ* Japan or Australia, out by Atlantic and home by Suez Canal, or *vice versâ*, price **£125.** See "Round-the-World" Folder, supplied free.

AUSTRALIA AND NEW ZEALAND.—New Fast Passenger Route, *viâ* Vancouver.—Many optional routes, including Niagara Falls. Break of journey allowed.

Steamships of Canadian **Australian Line, largest, fastest, and finest** running from American Continent **to Australasia,** leave Vancouver monthly, calling at Victoria, B.C., Honolulu, Suva (Fiji), and Sydney. Electric light, good cuisine, exceptionally large cabins.

SUMMER TOURS.—Express Train Service to fishing and shooting grounds through the finest scenery in the world—an enchanting panorama of Lakes, Prairies, Mountains, and Rivers. The Dining Cars attached to all through trains are the crowning point in the luxury of travel. Hotels in the Rocky Mountains.

Everyone who reads this should apply personally or by letter for gratuitous and post-free accurate Maps and Handsomely-Illustrated Guide Books. Various sets of Pamphlets, describing services, &c., as above, are published. State which set is required.

CANADIAN PACIFIC RAILWAY,
67 and 68, KING WILLIAM STREET, LONDON, E.C.;
30, COCKSPUR STREET, CHARING CROSS, S.W.;
7, JAMES STREET, LIVERPOOL;
67, ST. VINCENT STREET, GLASGOW.

WESTERN  AUSTRALIA.

Conditions on which Land may be obtained from the Crown.

FREE HOMESTEAD FARMS.

Certain well chosen areas in the South-Western Division of the Colony are set apart by Government within which Free Farms may be selected, up to 160 acres, by anyout over 18 years of age not already holding over 100 acres of land in the Colony. The conditions are:—The selector shall pay £1 deposit on application and reside on the block, and make it his usual home during at least six months in each year for the first five years, and shall within two years either erect a habitable house to the value of not less than £30 ; or, in lieu thereof, expend an equal amount in clearing and cropping a portion of his holding ; or he may, in lieu thereof, properly prepare and plant two acres of orchard or vineyard. And further, within five years from the date of possession, the selector must fence in at least one-fourth of his holding, and clear and crop one-eighth ; and within seven years of same date must clear and crop one-fourth of his holding, and fence the whole of it ; and upon the due completion of such improvements shall obtain the Crown grant.

HOMESTEAD LEASES OR GRAZING FARMS.

Within the South-Western Division, and also if within 40 miles of a railway in the Eucla and Eastern Divisions, areas of the second and third class lands of the Colony are being classed, proclaimed, and set apart for selection on the following conditions, viz.:—In respect of second class lands, any person over 18 years may select not less than 1000 acres or more than 3000 acres ; and for third class lands, not less than 1000 or more than 5000 acres, to be held on the following terms and conditions:—He shall, for second class land, pay rent for 30 years, at the rate of 2d. per acre per annum for first 15 years, and 3d. per acre per annum for next 15 years ; and for third class lands, 1d. per acre for 15 years, and 2d. for next 15 years. He shall, by himself or an agent, or servant, reside on the holding during nine months in each year for the first five years, and shall execute the following improvements, viz :—During first two years fence one-half of his holding, and during following two years fence the whole of it, and, in addition to the fencing, expend during the first 15 years of his lease, in statutory improvements, an amount equal to 6s. 8d. per acre in respect of second class lands, and 4s. 2d. per acre per annum for third class lands. Such improvements may consist of either subdivision, fences, clearing, cultivating, grubbing, draining, ringbarking, tanks, dams, wells, and any other work which will improve the productiveness of the land. Upon completion of payments and improvements a Crown grant shall issue.

CONDITIONAL PURCHASES.

The conditions of settlement and tenure for first class lands, in South-Western Division, are as follows :—

Any person over 18 years of age may take up from 100 to 1000 acres for 6d. per acre per annum for 20 years ; during the first five years he must reside upon the land for at least six months in each year—within two years he must fence in one-tenth, and within five years the whole of the land, and within ten years he must, in addition, expend on the land an amount equal to 10s. per acre in *bonâ fide* improvements ;

Orchard blocks. Or he may take up a vineyard and orchard lot of from 5 to 20 acres, by paying £1 per acre cash, and during first three years the land must be fenced, and at least one-tenth planted with vines and fruit trees or as a vegetable garden ;

Free purchase lots. Or he may purchase (if not within a declared agricultural area) from 100 up to 5000 acres, or within an agricultural area from 100 to 1000 acres, paying 10s. per acre cash, and within three years shall fence it in, and within seven years expend to the amount of 5s. per acre in prescribed improvements.

PASTORAL LEASES.

Land in the Kimberley, North-West, Gascoyne, and Eucla Divisions may be leased in blocks of not less than 20,000 acres, for 10s. per thousand per annum ; or in the Eastern Division for 2s. 6d. per thousand acres per annum. In the South-Western Division a minimum area of 1000 acres is allowed, the rent being £1 per thousand acres ; but in this division no security of tenure is given as against free selection, except that purchasers have to pay the pastoral lessee the fair value of any improvements made by such lessee.

The term of all pastoral leases expires on 31st December, 1907.

A. R. RICHARDSON, *Commissioner of Crown Lands.*